ME, ME, ME (Moi)

I0139503

Eugène Labiche
&
Èdouard Martin

translated by
Laurence Senelick

BROADWAY PLAY PUBLISHING INC
New York
www.broadwayplaypublishing.com
info@broadwayplaypublishing.com

ME, ME, ME
© Copyright 2018 Laurence Senelick

All rights reserved. This work is fully protected under the copyright laws of the United States of America. No part of this publication may be photocopied, reproduced, stored in a retrieval system, or transmitted, in any form or by any means, electronic, mechanical, recording, or otherwise, without the prior permission of the publisher. Additional copies of this play are available from the publisher.

Written permission is required for live performance of any sort. This includes readings, cuttings, scenes, and excerpts. For amateur and stock performances, please contact Broadway Play Publishing Inc. For all other rights please contact the translator c/o B P P I.

Cover art *L'Egoïsme personnifié (Selfishness Personified)*

First edition: August 2018
I S B N: 978-0-88145-789-6

Book design: Marie Donovan
Page make-up: Adobe InDesign
Typeface: Palatino

First performed at the Théâtre Français, Paris,
21 March 1864.

CHARACTERS

DUTRÉCY, *a man of means*
ARMAND BERNIER, *his nephew*
THÉRÈSE, *his niece*
DE LA PORCHERAIE, *another man of means*
FROMENTAL, *a banker*
GEORGES FROMENTAL, *his son*
MADAME DE VERRIÈRES, *his widowed daughter*
FOURCINIER, *a medical doctor*
AUBIN, DUTRÉCY'*s valet*
CYPRIEN, DUTRÉCY'*s valet*
GERMAIN, DUTRÉCY'*s valet*

[Translator's note: CYPRIEN *and* GERMAIN *appear only in* ACT ONE; *they may be doubled with the servants in* ACT TWO.]

The scene is set in Paris around 1864. ACT ONE *and* ACT THREE, *at* DUTRÉCY'*s home;* ACT TWO, *at* FROMENTAL'*s.*

ACT ONE

(DUTRÉCY's *home*)

(AUBIN, CYPRIEN *and* GERMAIN *enter.*)

CYPRIEN: Has the water heater been lit?

GERMAIN: Yes, first thing this morning.

CYPRIEN: Good… Let's have a look at the thermometer… Sixty degrees; that's the norm.

GEORGES: *(Appearing at back)* Monsieur Dutrécy?

CYPRIEN: That's right…but the master is not available right now…

GEORGES: And Monsieur Armand Bernier, his nephew?

GERMAIN: *(Astonished)* His nephew?

CYPRIEN: That's a new one on us.

GERMAIN: The master has only a niece…Mademoiselle Thérèse, who's away at boarding school…

GEORGES: Yes…I know. *(Aside)* Armand hasn't arrived yet. *(Aloud)* At what time does Monsieur Dutrècy receive visitors?

CYPRIEN: Why…around noon.

GEORGES: All right… *(Aside)* My father and my sister will have time to see him…and today my fate will be sealed.

CYPRIEN: Would the gentleman care to leave his name?

GEORGES: There's no point...I'll be back. *(He exits.)*

GERMAIN: Who is that gentleman?

CYPRIEN: It's the first time I've seen him. *(Looking at his watch.)* Watch out! The master may ring at any minute.

AUBIN: *(Pointing to the right)* What's the master doing in there?

CYPRIEN: Hydrotherapy.

AUBIN: What did you say? Hydro...

CYPRIEN: Right! You can tell this fellow's just in yesterday from the wilds of Brittany...

GERMAIN: With hair like that!

CYPRIEN: *(To* AUBIN, *pompously)* My good man, hydrotherapy is what they call a tank made of zinc, beneath which the master stands in a state of nature; when the master decides he is sufficiently damp, he rings the first time...that'll be for you.

AUBIN: For me?

CYPRIEN: You will go in and rub him down with a towel as coarse and rough as a cheese-grater, until he turns bright red...

GERMAIN: That's to bring on a reaction...

CYPRIEN: When he's done, the master will ring a second time...that's Germain's turn.

GERMAIN: *(Indicating a tray on the table)* I come in with that...a glass of Madeira and two wafers...that completes the reaction.

AUBIN: It's all so well arranged...

CYPRIEN: Ah! it's because Monsieur Dutrécy understands the meaning of life! ...He knows how to take care of himself, he does.

AUBIN: Is his health poorly?

CYPRIEN: Him! He's a fresh as a rose! ...And yet, when one of his horses turns a hair, he calls in three doctors for a consultation.

(A bell rings at right.)

GERMAIN: First bell!

CYPRIEN: That's you, Aubin! ...Go, quick! And don't spare the elbow-grease...

AUBIN: Don't worry...I've curry-combed horses for five years...I'll give him a proper rubdown... *(He goes off right.)*

GERMAIN: What possessed the master to hire that clod?

CYPRIEN: A peasant is...sturdy, he can rub for a very long time. *(A bell rings at right.)* Second bell!

GERMAIN: *(Taking the tray from the table)* For the Madeira! *(He quickly goes off right.)*

LA PORCHERAIE: *(Offstage)* Never mind...don't announce me! *(He appears.)*

CYPRIEN: Monsieur de la Porcheraie.

LA PORCHERAIE: Good morning, Cyprien...where's Dutrécy?

CYPRIEN: The master is having his shower bath.

LA PORCHERAIE: Nine-thirty... Right on cue!

CYPRIEN: Would Monsieur care to be announced?

LA PORCHERAIE: No point...I'll wait... Ah! would you happen to have a map of the rebuilding of Paris?

CYPRIEN: There's one lying open on the master's desk.

LA PORCHERAIE: *(Astonished)* Open?

CYPRIEN: The master was poring over it for more than an hour when he got back last night.

LA PORCHERAIE: *(Aside)* Well, well! ...Have we had the same idea? That would be funny. *(Aloud)* Come on, show me in.

CYPRIEN: This way, Monsieur...

(They both go off left.)

AUBIN: *(Entering)* Well, he should be satisfied! I rubbed him down... He kept saying, harder! Harder! I was afraid I'd skin him alive!

DUTRÉCY: *(Entering, his face beaming)* Ah! I feel good, I feel toned up...my muscles are supple, my skin is doing its job. *(Noticing AUBIN)* Ah! there you are... come over here, my boy!

AUBIN: *(Coming closer)* Monsieur...

DUTRÉCY: My good fellow, I am pleased with you... You're pretty good at rubdowns... Your movements are not yet rhythmical enough...but that'll come! Tell me...was I bright red...on my backside?

AUBIN: Ah! Monsieur...I didn't look...

DUTRÉCY: Next time, be so kind as to take a look...it's most important...the bottom is crucial! ...Well...are you getting used to Paris?

AUBIN: Shucks! I only been out the once to call you a cab... *(Fumbling in his pocket)* By the way I got to give you back five sous.

DUTRÉCY: Five sous!

AUBIN: It was the coachman... When I found him at his stand, he said, "Here's your five sous".

DUTRÉCY: And you're giving them back to me?

AUBIN: Sure thing.

DUTRÉCY: *(Aside)* How generous! Oh, innocent Brittany! *(Aloud)* My good man...you've done a good deed... keep them! ...To get your hair cut.

AUBIN: If the master don't mind, I'll cut it myself...

DUTRÉCY: As you wish... *(Aside)* He's thrifty, honest.
Here's an idea! *(Aloud)* Aubin!

AUBIN: Monsieur?

DUTRÉCY: I'm going to give you a great proof of my
confidence...I am as jealous as a lover about my
wine cellar; so far I have always gone down there
myself... It's not very wise to go down there, because
you're warm when you go in, you suddenly change
temperature...and bingo! inflammation of the lungs...
which could kill you! ...My good fellow, you shall go
in my place.

AUBIN: If the master pleases...

DUTRÉCY: *(Aside)* Splendid! Someone else would have
jumped for joy... Oh! innocent Brittany! *(Aloud)* Ah!
an instruction about the wine! ...I almost always have
some friend to lunch or dinner, the doctor advises
it...you don't rush through the meal and then it's
beneficial for the stomach... Now, I have two kinds of
wine, listen to me carefully, one has a red seal, that's a
Côtes Destourmel, 1846, a medicinal wine...I keep that
for myself...the other, green seal, is a sound claret...
which doesn't agree with me as well...you will pour
the green seal for my friends...the red seal you will
serve only to me...me alone...without anyone being
aware, of course.

AUBIN: Yes, Monsieur.

DUTRÉCY: It has nothing to do with the cost...but I have
no more than sixty-two bottles left... So, of course...

AUBIN: Yes, Monsieur, the good for you and the bad for
your friends.

DUTRÉCY: It isn't bad! ...It's a `58...if it were bad I
wouldn't serve it...it's a little less mellow...it's a wine
for guests.

CYPRIEN: *(Entering left and speaking offstage)* Yes, Monsieur...I shall inform him!...

DUTRÉCY: Cyprien... Whom were you addressing just now?

CYPRIEN: Monsieur de la Porcheraie who is in your study...

DUTRÉCY: What! My dear friend is in there...why didn't you show him in here?

CYPRIEN: He asked if the master had a map of the rebuilding of Paris...

DUTRÉCY: *(Surprised)* A map!

CYPRIEN: Here comes Monsieur de la Porcheraie.

LA PORCHERAIE: *(Entering left)* Good morning, dear friend.

DUTRÉCY: Good morning!... *(Aside)* Can we have had the same idea? ...that's not funny... *(To* AUBIN *and* CYPRIEN*)* All right...leave us.

*(*AUBIN *and* CYPRIEN *exit right.)*

LA PORCHERAIE: Do sit down.

DUTRÉCY: But what were you doing so early in my study?

LA PORCHERAIE: I was collecting information... Yesterday, at the Opera, I was with you in your box, during the ballet...

DUTRÉCY: Yes...

LA PORCHERAIE: You were watching the exertions of the ballerinas...while I was listening...

DUTRÉCY: *(Anxious)* Ah! to the music.

LA PORCHERAIE: To a gentleman in the next box who struck me as having all sorts of reasons for being well

informed…this gentleman was saying that they're
going to put through a new street…

DUTRÉCY: *(Quickly)* In Passy…through the garden of Dr
Fourcinier?

LA PORCHERAIE: So you were eavesdropping too! The
garden is four acres …

DUTRÉCY: At least!

LA PORCHERAIE: And if one could buy the property
before news got about… One might make a hundred
thousand crowns…I'm thinking of pulling off this little
deal…

DUTRÉCY: *(Quickly)* Ah! if you don't mind, I'm thinking
of it too.

LA PORCHERAIE: What! you're following in my
footsteps…

DUTRÉCY: Excuse me! you're following in mine…the
deal belongs to me first.

LA PORCHERAIE: Why?

DUTRÉCY: You were in my box when you heard the
news.

LA PORCHERAIE: Come off it! A word dropped in my
ear, and my ear has nothing to do with your box.

DUTRÉCY: At the very least it's a matter of common
courtesy…

LA PORCHERAIE: Oh! no fine phrases! …We're talking
business…

DUTRÉCY: And yet…look here…listen to me…you can't
behave like this…you! A friend of ten years! …Whose
hand I shake every day…

LA PORCHERAIE: Well, don't I shake your hand too? A
handshake…what does that prove?

DUTRÉCY: What?

LA PORCHERAIE: It proves we know one another…a bit. We live the same life, we belong to the same club, you love good things…I love exquisite things. We have the same tastes…and probably the same vices.

DUTRÉCY: Most kind of you!

LA PORCHERAIE: You're rich, I have an annual income of forty thousand livres… We are sure that we will never borrow money from one another…so, shake on it!

DUTRÉCY: Not so fast!

LA PORCHERAIE: But if that makes you think I'm going to sacrifice a lucrative deal on the altar of friendship! … No, I'm not your man any more…I withdraw my hand!

DUTRÉCY: *(Aside)* Actually he's right! *(Aloud)* Come, come, my dear friend, let's drop it…proceed with the deal…go ahead and make an offer…

LA PORCHERAIE: You give it up?

DUTRÉCY: Oh, I didn't say that!

LA PORCHERAIE: What then?

DUTRÉCY: I reserve the right to compete with you…to up your bid…

LA PORCHERAIE: All right! What you've just said makes sense… Now let's talk it over…

DUTRÉCY: Do have a seat.

LA PORCHERAIE: No, thank you.

DUTRÉCY: As you like.

LA PORCHERAIE: Come now…would you like to be partners in the deal?

DUTRÉCY: Frankly, I'd prefer to do it all by myself.

LA PORCHERAIE: Blast it! so would I! …But since there's no way…

DUTRÉCY: True enough…all right, I accept! Give me
your hand!…

LA PORCHERAIE: Our friendship turns out to be on
good terms with our self-interest…so…

DUTRÉCY: So…your hand on it…

LA PORCHERAIE: Your hand on it.

(DUTRÉCY *and* LA PORCHERAIE *shake hands.*)

DUTRÉCY: It's wonderful how we agree.

LA PORCHERAIE: We are two minds with but a single
thought… The first time I saw you, I immediately
appreciated you… We were in the front compartment
of a stage-coach…

DUTRÉCY: The Toulouse road… There were still stage-
coaches in those days…

LA PORCHERAIE: We were alone…we each took up a
corner.

DUTRÉCY: And your overnight bag was in the middle…
which considerably annoyed me…

LA PORCHERAIE: I like to stretch my legs…I am like
you… At one of the relay stations a lady got in…rather
pretty for that part of the country…you didn't budge,
you closed your eyes and kept to your corner.

DUTRÉCY: So did you!

LA PORCHERAIE: Indeed I did! So I said to myself:
That's a strong-minded man! That's a man who knows
what's what! And I conceived a certain respect for you.

DUTRÉCY: My dear friend, you're mistaken…I know
what's due to ladies…but I was feeling ill…I was
sleeping.

LA PORCHERAIE: Come off it! at least I have the courage
of my convictions. If I didn't give my seat to that lady,

it was because I was very comfortable in my corner and would have been very badly off in the middle!

DUTRÉCY: Not another word! You're nothing but an egotist!

LA PORCHERAIE: I believe we're both members of the same family...

DUTRÉCY: Really! ...I may have my faults...but not that...I think it's appalling!

LA PORCHERAIE: Do you know the difference between us? ...You are a timid egotist...a rose-colored egotist...I have saved the cost of pink dye, I have kept my natural color...

DUTRÉCY: *(Aside)* He is monstrous! *(Aloud)* Are you lunching with me?

LA PORCHERAIE: Impossible! I have another invitation.

DUTRÉCY: Well, you'll be the loser... Please stay...

LA PORCHERAIE: Let's see...tell me frankly—what're you having for lunch?

DUTRÉCY: Greedy gut!—A truffled partridge!...well, chubby?

LA PORCHERAIE: At the other place there's a woodcock ragout... What else?

DUTRÉCY: Hothouse asparagus...big stalks!

LA PORCHERAIE: At the other place, baby green peas...I am in a fix.

DUTRÉCY: Well, yesterday, as I went by Chevet's, I noticed a little melon...

LA PORCHERAIE: Why, I haven't eaten any this year... I'll lunch with you!

DUTRÉCY: So it's not on my account...but the melon's.

LA PORCHERAIE: Let's be honest…you invite me, because you're bored when you eat alone.

DUTRÉCY: *(Forgetting himself)* Yes… *(Recovering.)* I mean no…

LA PORCHERAIE: I accept…because your lunch is the better one…

DUTRÉCY: How polite!

(DUTRÉCY rings. AUBIN appears.)

DUTRÉCY: Set one more place and tell them to serve lunch punctually.

LA PORCHERAIE: *(Looking at AUBIN through his eyeglass)* Where the devil did you dig up that valet?

DUTRÉCY: He's all right, isn't he? He's from Brittany…a honest fellow…devoted…it's in their nature.

LA PORCHERAIE: I treated myself to one once upon a time…a heart of gold! …Unfortunately he would wear my boots…it's annoying when someone from Brittany with big feet wears your boots…

AUBIN: *(To DUTRÉCY)* Monsieur…I have a letter for you in my pocket.

DUTRÉCY: Well, hand it over!

AUBIN: *(Pulling it from his pocket)* Here it is!

DUTRÉCY: All right…lunch right away…

(AUBIN exits.)

DUTRÉCY: *(Opening the letter.)* Ah, it's from Armand…

LA PORCHERAIE: Your nephew…

DUTRÉCY: The boy I brought up…for I do bring up children…that's not so bad…for an egotist. Why, he's in Brazil.

LA PORCHERAIE: You didn't know?

DUTRÉCY: I did not! ...With sailors you never know where they are. *(Reading)* "My dear uncle, I write you sitting on the bed of a friend who is down with yellow fever..." *(Stops reading and holding the letter at a distance)* My friend, I don't know what's wrong with my spectacles...do me the kindness of carrying on.

(DUTRÉCY offers LA PORCHERAIE the letter.)

LA PORCHERAIE: *(Taking it)* There's nothing to fear... they dip them in vinegar. *(Reading)* "Down with yellow fever...I am the only one to care for him, this is to tell you that I shall stay with him to the last."

DUTRÉCY: Careless boy!

LA PORCHERAIE: Imbecile! *(Reading)* "I do not know what fate awaits me...if I do not see you again...accept my thanks for all the care you took for my childhood and the friendship you have always shown me."

DUTRÉCY: Yes, poor boy!

LA PORCHERAIE: *(Reading)* "Tell my dear cousin Thérèse that my last memory will be of her."

DUTRÉCY: The date! The date of the letter!

LA PORCHERAIE: On board the Brazilian ship *La Fiorina*, September twenty-fifth.

DUTRÉCY: Five months ago!...

LA PORCHERAIE: *(Handing him back the letter)* In vinegar!

DUTRÉCY: And no news since then! It's over! I shall never see him again!...

LA PORCHERAIE: Oh, who knows!

DUTRÉCY: I tell you I'll never see him again! It's awful!

LA PORCHERAIE: *(Aside)* He thinks he has to cry...I'm sorry I didn't pick the other lunch...

DUTRÉCY: A boy I always cared for...a boy who... He was supposed to bring me cigars from Havana!...

LA PORCHERAIE: Oh! the ones the government monopoly sells are first-rate!...

DUTRÉCY: It pains me...

LA PORCHERAIE: *(Taking his hat)* Come, come! You are in the dumps...I shall definitely not have lunch with you.

DUTRÉCY: What! You're leaving me?

LA PORCHERAIE: I'll be back soon...great sorrows require solitude! ...Good-bye!...

*(*LA PORCHERAIE *is about to exit as* CYPRIEN *enters.)*

CYPRIEN: Monsieur, Doctor Fourcinier is in the drawing-room.

LA PORCHERAIE: Fourcinier!

DUTRÉCY: *(Quickly)* The garden! Show him in!

*(*CYPRIEN *exits.)*

DUTRÉCY: Don't go away!

LA PORCHERAIE: No...you had better see the doctor on your own...you can talk to him casually about his garden, it will put him off his guard...besides, people place their confidence in a show of sympathy... You can tell him that it's a bad piece of property...

DUTRÉCY: Yes...taxes and no revenue!

LA PORCHERAIE: For the rest, trust to me! ...Silence! Here he is!

FOURCINIER: *(Appears)* Gentlemen!

DUTRÉCY: Why, it's the doctor!

LA PORCHERAIE: Good morning, Doctor!

DUTRÉCY: What good wind blows you here?

FOURCINIER: Today is Wednesday... Don't I come every Wednesday to ascertain the state of your health?

DUTRÉCY: Quite right. I forgot it's Wednesday.

FOURCINIER: How are we today?

DUTRÉCY: Not too bad.

LA PORCHERAIE: You're having a consultation...I'll leave you... Ah! Doctor, I'll have to consult you as well, my stomach is acting up.

FOURCINIER: Bloat...caused by overeating...

LA PORCHERAIE: What a sharp diagnosis! Shall I expect you tomorrow at my place?

FOURCINIER: Four o'clock!

LA PORCHERAIE: Four o'clock! *(Undertone to* DUTRÉCY*)* If you play your cards right, the game is ours.

DUTRÉCY: *(Undertone)* Don't worry!

LA PORCHERAIE: *(Exits)* Four o'clock then.

FOURCINIER: Let's have a look...the pulse is good...the hand is cool...the eye is keen...there's nothing for me to do...till next Wednesday!

DUTRÉCY: Wait a minute! That can't count as a visit!... *(Aside)* and the garden!

FOURCINIER: By the way, have you had a visit from Fromental and Madame de Verrières?

DUTRÉCY: No...Fromental...a classmate from Saint-Barbe! ...We've met a few times since graduation...but we don't see one another on a regular basis... What can he want of me?

FOURCINIER: He'll tell you himself...I'm in haste today.

(Seeing AUBIN *enter with a laden platter:)*

FOURCINIER: Why, here's your lunch...I'll leave you.

DUTRÉCY: Come now, Doctor...off the cuff, have lunch with me?

FOURCINIER: Oh no! I never eat lunch...a cup of tea on the run...

DUTRÉCY: *(Uncovering a dish)* Doctor, have a look at this...

FOURCINIER: It's a partridge.

DUTRÉCY: With truffles!...

FOURCINIER: *(Hesitating)* The fact is...they're waiting for me... *(Looking at his watch)* Well now...I can't give you more than five minutes...

DUTRÉCY: *(Aside)* That'll be enough...I've got him! *(Aloud)* Let's sit down!

(DUTRÉCY and FOURCINIER take their places at the table.)

FOURCINIER: And let's not dawdle.

DUTRÉCY: Doctor...spring is here...everyone advises me to go to the country... What do you think?

FOURCINIER: *(Eating very quickly)* Good idea! Very good idea!

DUTRÉCY: There's mention of Auteuil...or Passy...

FOURCINIER: Pick Passy...it's got a better exposure.

DUTRÉCY: *(Aside)* Naturally. *(Aloud)* Is it a pretty spot?

FOURCINIER: Oh, charming, charming! It gets better every day...the building lots around there are increasing in value... *(To AUBIN)* Let me have something to drink.

AUBIN: *(Undertone to DUTRÉCY)* Monsieur, I can't remember... Does he get the green seal?

DUTRÉCY: *(Undertone)* Yes, the green!

(AUBIN, who is holding two bottles, puts the bottle with the red seal under his arm and pours the green seal for FOURCINIER.)

FOURCINIER: Thank you...

(FOURCINIER *drinks and makes a face. He notices* AUBIN *put the green seal under his arm and pour out red seal to* DUTRÉCY)

FOURCINIER: *(Aside)* Well, well, to each his own bottle!

DUTRÉCY: *(Aside, after having drunk)* It's amazing how well this wine sets me up! *(Aloud)* Doctor, you're not drinking… *(To* AUBIN) Pour it out!

(AUBIN *takes up the green seal under his arm and is about to pour for* FOURCINIER.)

FOURCINIER: *(Stopping him)* No, not that one!… *(Indicating the red seal.)* The other one!

AUBIN: *(To* DUTRÉCY) Should I, Monsieur?

DUTRÉCY: Certainly… *(To* FOURCINIER.) But you won't like it.

FOURCINIER: Let me have it anyway.

DUTRÉCY: It's the wine you told me to take with an infusion of quinine…

FOURCINIER: *(Slowly savors the wine from the red-seal bottle and says to* AUBIN) My good fellow, in future you shall always serve me the quinine wine.

DUTRÉCY: Ah!

FOURCINIER: Well considered.

DUTRÉCY: So you advise me to pick Passy…

FOURCINIER: Certainly… It's a forest primeval…a basket of flowers…

DUTRÉCY: I was hesitating because…there's a good chance a central slaughter-house is going up there…

FOURCINIER: *(Stops eating)* What! A slaughter-house!

DUTRÉCY: It's a serious project…I was offered shares in the company…

FOURCINIER: But where is it? Which district?

DUTRÉCY: *(Pretending to search)* Wait a minute…rue… rue des Dames, I believe…

FOURCINIER: Goodness! …That's my land!

DUTRÉCY: You have property there?

FOURCINIER: Four acres…

DUTRÉCY: The slaughter-house will occupy number 9.

FOURCINIER: I'm 10…

DUTRÉCY: Then, it's across the way…that shouldn't be a problem.

FOURCINIER: No! No!

DUTRÉCY: Only it's tiresome to hear the cattle lowing… for the ladies!…and then in summer…the smells, the flies, the emanations!…

FOURCINIER: *(Quickly)* That's not unhealthy! *(He rises.)*

DUTRÉCY: You haven't touched your asparagus!

FOURCINIER: Thanks…I'm done. *(Aside)* A slaughter-house.

DUTRÉCY: *(Aside)* Got him!

FOURCINIER: *(Taking his hat)* Excuse me! I forgot…I really don't have the time.

DUTRÉCY: Yes…your patients…a sacred duty.

FOURCINIER: *(Aside)* Exactly…I'll run over to the town hall…I have a patient in the planning office.

CYPRIEN: *(Appearing)* Madame de Verrières and Monsieur Fromental wonder if Monsieur would care to receive them?

DUTRÉCY: *(Quickly)* Wait! I don't know if I'm at home…

FOURCINIER: What do you mean?

DUTRÉCY: Solicitations! …You can't imagine!…

FOURCINIER: Fromental?

DUTRÉCY: You see, there's a calamity in my family…I have a cousin four times removed who had the bad luck to be appointed secretary general of a government committee…so now they assume that I'm going to find jobs for all the Saint-Barbe alumni!…

FOURCINIER: But you've got it all wrong…Fromental's request won't cost you the least effort…

DUTRÉCY: You're sure?

FOURCINIER: Quite sure!

DUTRÉCY: But I can't receive them in an outfit like this.

FOURCINIER: Don't worry, they are forewarned…I gave out that you are ill…

DUTRÉCY: Thanks…ask them to come in…

FOURCINIER: I can't run into them…it would make me late… *(Indicating a side door)* I'll slip out through there.

DUTRÉCY: Wait! At least tell me what they want of me.

FOURCINIER: If you must know, it has to do with a marriage.

DUTRÉCY: For me?

FOURCINIER: For your niece.

DUTRÉCY: What niece?

FOURCINIER: Good grief! You have only one… Thérèse…who's at boarding school.

DUTRÉCY: Ah! that's right! the dear child!…

FOURCINIER: He forgot about her! What a man!… *(He exits at the side.)*

DUTRÉCY: *(Alone)* A marriage! Now all the family nuisances are starting…my lunch interrupted…my appetite spoiled… Clear the table… Interviews! … Introductions… Well, if it has to be done, I want it to be done as soon as possible.

(FROMENTAL *and* MME DE VERRIÈRES *appear at the back introduced by* CYPRIEN *who exits.)*

FROMENTAL: My dear classmate…I've long been eager to come and shake your hand.

DUTRÉCY: My dear Fromental! *(They shake hands.)*

FROMENTAL: Allow me to introduce my daughter… widow of Colonel de Verrières.

DUTRÉCY: *(Bowing)* Madame, the doctor told me that you have been forewarned…my invalid's outfit… please be seated…

(AUBIN *offers seats and exits.)*

FROMENTAL: My dear classmate…we very rarely meet…

DUTRÉCY: Quite true; we see one another every ten or fifteen years.

FROMENTAL: It's somewhat your fault…you never come to our Saint-Barbe reunion dinners…

DUTRÉCY: Oh, you know…those dinners…

FROMENTAL: Are full of conviviality… They read out verses.

MME DE VERRIÈRES: Father…

FROMENTAL: That's right…I'll come to the reason for our visit… My dear classmate…I have a son… A Saint-Barbian, same as us! …Georges…that's his name, back from America yesterday… He had undertaken the journey to call on the investors in our banking house… and I may say he succeeded beyond all our hopes… He is a very shrewd businessman…

MME DE VERRIÈRES: And what's even better, he has a heart…he is dependable and honest in his relations…

FROMENTAL: In short, before he left, he had been attracted to Mademoiselle Thérèse, your niece.

DUTRÉCY: Really? ...But where could he have seen her? ...She never leaves her boarding school!...

MME DE VERRIÈRES: At the home of one of our mutual friends, Madame de Puysole...whom you authorized to take Thérèse home for the holidays.

DUTRÉCY: True enough...I couldn't have her here...a bachelor...

FROMENTAL: We have come to ask...frankly...if you have any objections to the union that my children and I have long desired...

DUTRÉCY: Goodness me! ...You've caught me somewhat unprepared...I'm very fond of Thérèse... And I won't conceal from you that the idea of a separation... However, if your son succeeds in winning her over...

MME DE VERRIÈRES: Oh, I don't believe we'll have any resistance on that side.

FROMENTAL: Georges' position is a handsome one... He has a third share in my bank's profits... What's more, I'll give him four hundred thousand francs.

DUTRÉCY: Thérèse, for her part...

FROMENTAL: Three hundred and twenty-eight thousand francs...I know...

DUTRÉCY: (Astonished) What?

FROMENTAL: We have the same notary...Frémicourt... He's a Saint-Barbian!...

DUTRÉCY: Ah! all right...

MME DE VERRIÈRES: My brother, Monsieur, is very eager to meet you... If you would allow us to return...

DUTRÉCY: Whenever you like...the interview can take place this very day...

FROMENTAL: Today?...

MME DE VERRIÈRES: Around three o'clock, would that suit you?...

DUTRÉCY: Very good!... *(Changing his mind)* Ah! blast! ...It's that...I have to go and pick up Thérèse at the school...and it's far away...the school...

MME DE VERRIÈRES: Don't worry about that...Madame de Puysole is authorized to take her out... She can collect her on your behalf and bring her to you here...

DUTRÉCY: Perfect! ...That's perfect! ...Then I think this marriage will proceed very swiftly.

MME DE VERRIÈRES: My brother won't be the one to brook any delays.

DUTRÉCY: Nor will I...because once a thing is settled... and besides, I can't keep a young lady in my house... you understand...a bachelor!...

MME DE VERRIÈRES: We still have to wait two weeks.

FROMENTAL: Let's say a month.

DUTRÉCY: Why a month?

FROMENTAL: The time it takes to publish the banns.

DUTRÉCY: Ah yes, the banns.... We'll have to traipse around mayors' offices...

MME DE VERRIÈRES: *(Quickly)* My father will take charge of the running around...

DUTRÉCY: Perfect! ...That's perfect!...

FROMENTAL: We shall then have think about renting them an apartment.

DUTRÉCY: Yes...an apartment.

MME DE VERRIÈRES: *(Quickly)* I know a delightful one... nearby...rue de Provence.

FROMENTAL: It has to be furnished.

MME DE VERRIÈRES: I have a decorator who works nights...

FROMENTAL: Finally, we'll have to buy the bridegroom's wedding gift, and the trousseau...

MME DE VERRIÈRES: I'll deal with that.

DUTRÉCY: Perfect! ...That's perfect! ...Furthermore, Madame, if you need me...I know nothing about all this...but I am at your disposal...

LA PORCHERAIE: *(Entering at the back)* Oof! ...I've just come from Passy!

FROMENTAL: Monsieur de la Porcheraie...

LA PORCHERAIE: *(Bowing)* Monsieur...Madame... What luck to run into you here! *(Undertone to DUTRÉCY)* Get rid of them...I have to talk to you about our deal...

DUTRÉCY: *(To FROMENTAL)* All right! ...Now that it's all settled...we've split up the work...

FROMENTAL: *(Bowing)* My dear classmate...till three o'clock!

DUTRÉCY: Three o'clock... As for my assignments...I shall be ready... *(Bowing to MME DE VERRIÈRES)* Madame...

(DUTRÉCY escorts them to the door at back.)

(FROMENTAL and MME DE VERRIÈRES exit.)

DUTRÉCY: *(Coming back to DE LA PORCHERAIE)* Well?

LA PORCHERAIE: I've seen the garden...splendid! ... What about Fourcinier? ...What did you tell him?

DUTRÉCY: I annihilated him...I've got him expecting a slaughterhouse to be built across from his front gate...

LA PORCHERAIE: Ah? Can you picture it? ...We need to exchange a little note to arrange our terms...

DUTRÉCY: I was planning to ask that of you as well.

LA PORCHERAIE: *(Unfolding a paper)* Naturally...I was accompanied by a surveyor and we drew up a map of the garden...

DUTRÉCY: Already?...

LA PORCHERAIE: Take a look at that...

DUTRÉCY: Let's see the street frontage...that's important...

LA PORCHERAIE: Three hundred and fifty-six yards... We shall carve a street down the middle and build villas on either side... Wait! ...I have a pencil...I'm going to mark them... *(He sits down at the table.)*

AUBIN: *(Entering)* Monsieur...there's a carriage stopping at the door.

DUTRÉCY: What do I care? ...I'm not at home!...

AUBIN: *(Looking out the window)* With trunks!...

DUTRÉCY: Trunks! ...I'm not expecting anyone!...

ARMAND: *(Appearing at back)* Not even me?

DUTRÉCY: Armand?... *(Stopping just before embracing him.)* You're cured, I hope?...

LA PORCHERAIE: *(Aside)* A heartfelt question!...

ARMAND: I've never even been sick...

(They embrace.)

ARMAND: Yellow fever would have nothing to do with me! ...And the friend I nursed disembarked with me two days ago at Saint-Nazaire...

DUTRÉCY: Ah! you can't imagine the anxiety, the concern... Did you bring me my cigars?

ARMAND: I did, and splendid ones at that! ...Planter's cigars...I have six boxes of them!...

DUTRÉCY: *(Indicating* DE LA PORCHERAIE*)* Hush! ...Not so loud...

ARMAND: He didn't hear, Monsieur de la Porcheraie!...

LA PORCHERAIE: Good afternoon, Armand... *(They shake hands.)* You can congratulate yourself on giving us a fright!... *(Looking at the map.)* May I?...

ARMAND: Uncle, may I abuse your hospitality for a while?

DUTRÉCY: You got a furlough?...

ARMAND: No, I handed in my resignation.

DUTRÉCY: What?...

ARMAND: You know I signed on to a Brazilian ship... One morning, as I wrote you, a case of yellow fever on board was announced...the Captain took advice and decided that the sick passenger should be left on the first beach we sighted...

LA PORCHERAIE: How well I understand that captain!...

ARMAND: I was outraged...I protested...but in vain... When I saw that poor creature lowered into a canoe, as if into a coffin...I couldn't contain myself...I tore off my epaulets and followed him!...

AUBIN: *(Who is setting the table at back, aside)* Ah! good for him!...

DUTRÉCY: What! You did that?...

LA PORCHERAIE: *(To* DUTRÉCY*)* So that's the way you bring up children!...

DUTRÉCY: But that's absurd! ...To hand in your resignation just to hook up with a man with yellow fever!...

ARMAND: Should I have abandoned him, alone... helpless, in a strange land? ...A fellow countryman? For I didn't tell you: he was a Frenchman!...

DUTRÉCY: For heaven's sake, it's not as if they're scarce! ...You could have found others... There are plenty of Frenchmen!...

LA PORCHERAIE: Armand, you make us grieve!...

ARMAND: I do?

LA PORCHERAIE: My friend, let me tell you, you are on a slippery slope...the slope of sacrifice which gave Don Quixote a bad name...

ARMAND: You would have done the same thing in my place!...

LA PORCHERAIE: Oh no I wouldn't!...

DUTRÉCY: I'll second that!...

LA PORCHERAIE: On occasions of supreme importance, I think of my *me*!...

ARMAND: What do you mean?

LA PORCHERAIE: That pretty little *me*...which forms our whole universe...

ARMAND: What in the world is your *me*?...

LA PORCHERAIE: It is a composite of all the organs that can give me pleasure...

AUBIN: *(Aside, eavesdropping)* He speaks well, the master's friend...

LA PORCHERAIE: It's my mouth...when it savors a tasty truffle, my eyes when they light on a pretty woman...

AUBIN: *(Aside, thrilled)* Oh, oh!

LA PORCHERAIE: My ear...when it brings me the sound of music...the kind that aids digestion and demands scant attention...

ARMAND: Well! ...What about the heart?...

LA PORCHERAIE: Oh, the heart doesn't live there...it's not one of the family...a noble stranger who can't be kicked out, unfortunately…but must be rigorously watched, lest he remove the bread from the mouth and toss our silverware out the window to the bystanders.

ARMAND: Uncle, have you nothing to say?

DUTRÉCY: I? …I am outraged! …When you speak to me of the heart…I will always be on your side…against de la Porcheraie… Yes, the heart is a noble organ…a gift from heaven! …Long may it reign…

LA PORCHERAIE: But not govern!…

DUTRÉCY: It's a constitutional monarch… *(To* ARMAND*)* You see, in this world…you mustn't be an egotist! …but you look after yourself, your fortune, your welfare…first of all, others won't look after them for you…

AUBIN: *(Aside)* The master's right…

DUTRÉCY: Remember what a wise man once said… all knowledge of life is contained in this: All oneself is never enough to look after oneself!…

AUBIN: *(Aside)* Why! …There's some red seal left! …The master is right: All oneself is never enough to look after myself! *(He hides the bottle under his coat and disappears.)*

ARMAND: And so, if I take your meaning, you would turn a man, a human being, into a kind of armor-plated, iron-clad fortress and write on the door, Me! … *Me alone!* …Well, we sailors see things with a different eye… You say: *me*… We say: *us*…of all our organs— (I borrow your term) the one we most esteem is the heart! …And it's not a guest we surveille…but a master whom we are proud to obey! …It is the master who teaches us the religion of devotion, who tells us that God created us weak so that we draw close to each other, love each another, help each another! …And it's that feeling of the brotherhood of all men that sailors respond to.

DUTRÉCY: Yes...it may be useful at sea, I don't deny it!

ARMAND: But, uncle, savages...savages themselves are aware of that human solidarity...

DUTRÉCY: Savages?...

ARMAND: Yes...judge for yourself: we landed in the midst of them, my dear patient and myself... First we were met with distrust, but when they saw that one of us was ailing, urged on by the holy law of compassion, they drew near, they opened their huts to us!...

LA PORCHERAIE: This is like a history of the Incas!...

ARMAND: When later I wanted to thank the leader of that little tribe...

LA PORCHERAIE: The big chief!...

ARMAND: He replied, "Man is indebted to man; once we lived in isolation and slept beneath the stars. One day one of us wanted to build a hut..."

LA PORCHERAIE: Uncle Tom's Cabin!...

ARMAND: "He cut down an oak; when the oak was on the ground, he realized that he was too weak to lift it; another man came by, he called to him and said, 'Help me. Carry my tree and I shall carry yours...'"

LA PORCHERAIE: And the Mutual Aid Society was born...capital in hand: one tree!...

DUTRÉCY: Say what you like...I find that fable very moving...and I would add that all men are brothers!...

LA PORCHERAIE: *(Aside)* Let's see where he's going with this...

DUTRÉCY: Each one of us, on this earth, must carry his neighbor's tree...yes!...

LA PORCHERAIE: Listen, I figure five villas on the left and four on the right...

DUTRÉCY: Why not five on each side?...

LA PORCHERAIE: Not enough air…it would be unhealthy!…

DUTRÉCY: *(Astonished)* Unhealthy? …But they're for sale!…

LA PORCHERAIE: *(Aside)* There! …He's dropped his tree!…

DUTRÉCY: Yes, humanity is a great forest…in which each tree…don't you agree?

LA PORCHERAIE: I don't own any forest land, I only have three per-cents in the funds!

DUTRÉCY: La Porcheraie, respect my convictions!…

LA PORCHERAIE: I'm going to get a ruler and a compass… *(To* ARMAND*)* No hard feelings! …We'll forgive you because you bring cigars!…

DUTRÉCY: *(Aside)* He heard!

ARMAND: Heartless cynic!

LA PORCHERAIE: Excuse me…but it is so funny, your little story about the savages… And you come and tell it in Paris, when the stock exchange is in session! …Why, you're a social heretic…your heresy is brotherhood. *(He goes off right.)*

ARMAND: And yours, Monsieur de la Porcheraie, is too little fellow-feeling!…

DUTRÉCY: Well said! …I was about to say so myself!

ARMAND: Now we are alone, let me have news of my cousin?

DUTRÉCY: Thérèse? …She's quite well!

ARMAND: She must be very grown-up, very beautiful…I haven't seen her for three years! …She was sixteen when I left…she was a child…but already so charming! …Such gentle seriousness! Such melancholy in her glance!…

DUTRÉCY: She's all right... You shall see her!...

ARMAND: How?

DUTRÉCY: This very day...I'm taking her out of boarding school!...

ARMAND: You're taking her out...forever?...

DUTRÉCY: Forever! ...I'm going to marry her off...

ARMAND: *(Moved)* Marry off Thérèse? ...To whom?...

DUTRÉCY: To a charming young man...full of heart... who has come from America.

ARMAND: *(Joyfully)* Ah! good heavens! ...Is it possible! ...That young man!...

DUTRÉCY: That young man has had Thérèse on his mind for a long time...and I believe that Thérèse, for her part... Ah! you weren't expecting that news?...

ARMAND: I must confess... *(Aside)* And I was accusing him of indifference...selfishness! ...Dear uncle! ... He was thinking of my happiness! ...I must be dreaming!...

DUTRÉCY: What's come over you?

ARMAND: Nothing! ...It's happiness...I so love Thérèse!...

DUTRÉCY: She's fond of you too, you know...

AUBIN: *(Entering. He is carrying trunks and six boxes of cigars)* Here's the gentleman's baggage... *(Aside)* Oof! ...Say what you like, this is one heavy family!...

ARMAND: Very good! ...Take it to my room...

AUBIN: The thing is...others have just arrived...

DUTRÉCY: What?

AUBIN: Yes...a young lady escorted by another lady... with a big case...

ARMAND: It's Thérèse!...

DUTRÉCY: My niece!…

ARMAND: What bliss! …I run to greet her!

AUBIN: *(To* ARMAND*)* But there's also a young man who already came this morning; he's waiting for you in your room…

ARMAND: A young man? …I can't see him at the moment…my cousin is here…his name?…

AUBIN: Monsieur Georges!… *(He exits.)*

ARMAND: Georges?… That's him, uncle!…

DUTRÉCY: Who him?…

ARMAND: The friend I saved!

DUTRÉCY: Well then? …Go and greet him…

ARMAND: But my cousin…

DUTRÉCY: You have plenty of time to see your cousin, since she'll be staying here…

ARMAND: You're right…I'll run and embrace Georges…and I'll come right back… It's as if he's arrived just in time to witness my happiness!… *(He exits.)*

*(*AUBIN *re-enters.)*

DUTRÉCY: *(To* AUBIN*)* You, go down and get my niece's trunks…

AUBIN: More trunks?… *(Aside)* What a house! …In the morning I rub down the master, at noon I scrub down the drawing-room…and now they're making me carry up trunks…I'll end up flat on my back…and shucks! … As the master says so well… You can never have too much of yourself…

DUTRÉCY: Well? …Didn't you hear me?

AUBIN: Yes, Monsieur… *(Aside)* It's too much! …much too much! …It can't go on like this!…

(AUBIN *exits at the moment* THÉRÈSE *appears.*)

THÉRÈSE: Good afternoon, uncle!...

DUTRÉCY: *(Embracing her)* Good afternoon, good afternoon... All alone?

THÉRÈSE: Madame de Puysole didn't want to come up... Ah! if you knew, uncle dearest, how nice it is to leave school!...

DUTRÉCY: *(Embracing her)* Yes...yes...I understand!... *(Aside)* Let's be the best of uncles...it's only for two weeks.

THÉRÈSE: I will never go back to Mademoiselle Pinta's school!...

DUTRÉCY: No!...

THÉRÈSE: What bliss!

DUTRÉCY: If you're going to get married, you have to be shown off...

THÉRÈSE: Get married?...

DUTRÉCY: Didn't Madame de Verrières tell you? ...A splendid match...Monsieur Georges Fromental...a Saint-Barbian...

THÉRÈSE: Ah!...

DUTRÉCY: You know him?

THÉRÈSE: *(Lowering her gaze)* Why...a little...

DUTRÉCY: You like him?...

THÉRÈSE: *(Hesitating)* But, uncle...

DUTRÉCY: Ah! my dear child, we must hurry, we have no time to lose... Do you like him, yes or no?...

(THÉRÈSE *lowers her gaze without replying.*)

DUTRÉCY: Very well! ...Silence means consent... You shall stay with me for two weeks...

THÉRÈSE: Two weeks?…

DUTRÉCY: It seems you can't get married in less time!…

THÉRÈSE: Oh! I'm going to be happy here… And you, uncle, are you glad to have me near you?

DUTRÉCY: Yes…yes…but first of all I have to inform you of my little habits!…

THÉRÈSE: You mustn't change anything for me, uncle!…

DUTRÉCY: I don't intend to… Sit down… This is my life: I get up at nine…I take a shower…I lunch at eleven on the dot…we wait for no one…too bad for those who aren't ready! …When I've had my coffee, I stretch out in this armchair…and I smoke my cigar… Perhaps you don't like the aroma of a cigar?…

THÉRÈSE: Oh! it doesn't matter to me, uncle!…

DUTRÉCY: Very good! …When I smoke, I don't speak! …And I prefer that no one speaks to me! …You can keep busy…but make no noise… At four o'clock, I ride on horseback to the Bois…when it rains, I take the buggy… You shall keep me company… We dine at six on the dot… Ah! a piece of advice! …No piano! …It puts me on edge!…

THÉRÈSE: (Smiling) That's easy enough, uncle!…

DUTRÉCY: So that's our little program… It can't be much fun for you, I suppose?…

THÉRÈSE: Oh! I never get bored!…

DUTRÉCY: Lucky you! …And now I'm going to give you a nice piece of news…Armand is here…

THÉRÈSE: My cousin?…

DUTRÉCY: He's a noble young man…who has lost his position… That means I have to play host to two individuals…I'd better let him know about my habits as well…

(ARMAND *appears.*)

THÉRÈSE: I hear him!… *(Undertone, to* DUTRÉCY) May I inform him of my marriage, uncle?

DUTRÉCY: If you like!… *(Noticing the boxes of cigars)* What about my cigars? …I mustn't let them lie about here!… *(He takes them.)* What if de la Porcheraie were to stop by!… *(To* THÉRÈSE) I leave you with your cousin… You're right…share your happiness with him… He loves you so much…he'll be pleased… *(He goes off right with the cigar boxes.)*

ARMAND: *(Moved)* Good afternoon, Thérèse! …Good afternoon, cousin!…

THÉRÈSE: Well! No hugs, Monsieur?

ARMAND: I don't dare…you've got so big!…

THÉRÈSE: You are so big…yourself! Come and hug me at once!

ARMAND: *(Embracing her)* How beautiful you are now!

THÉRÈSE: Think so? —And yet I'm still wearing my school uniform; but, you don't know, I'm never going back to Mademoiselle Pinta's…it's over!…

ARMAND: I do know!

THÉRÈSE: I have some other news to tell you… important news…I'm going to be married!

ARMAND: I know that too!

THÉRÈSE: Ah! how tiresome—you know everything! …But I'm so silly! …I haven't asked you how your journey was?…

ARMAND: Very pleasant! …Especially the return trip… This marriage doesn't frighten you?

THÉRÈSE: Not in the least! Quite the contrary!…

ARMAND: How good you are and how happy I am!...

THÉRÈSE: Happy?

ARMAND: Yes... very happy! I seem to be wallowing in happiness today...I see you again...and my best friend...whom I have found again...for he's here...in the next room!...

THÉRÈSE: What friend?

ARMAND: You don't know him.

GEORGES: *(Entering)* Armand! you're neglecting me.

ARMAND: I was just about to introduce you to him... Georges! *(Introducing him)* My cousin!

THÉRÈSE: Monsieur Fromental!...

ARMAND: You know one another?

THÉRÈSE: We certainly do.

GEORGES: Certainly.

ARMAND: *(Laughing)* And I was counting on introducing you to one another... *(Undertone to* GEORGES*)* Ah, my friend! if you only knew...I'm going to be married!...

GEORGES: *(Ditto)* Really! so am I!...

ARMAND: Honestly? ...Ah! what bliss! ...You shall be my best man! ...I shall be yours.

GEORGES: And you're in love?...

ARMAND: Madly!

GEORGES: So am I!...

ARMAND: And whom are you marrying?

AUBIN: *(Appearing with cardboard boxes and a big trunk on his shoulder, announcing with an ill grace)* Monsieur Fromental! Madame de Verrières! *(He disappears.)*

ARMAND: *(To* GEORGES*)* Your father!...

GEORGES: And my sister! ...You shall know it all!...

MME DE VERRIÈRES: *(Embracing* THÉRÈSE*)* My dear child!...

FROMENTAL: *(Bowing)* Mademoiselle...

GEORGES: Sister...father...Monsieur Armand Bernier... my very best friend!

FROMENTAL: *(Bowing)* Monsieur is no doubt a Saint-Barbian?

ARMAND: I haven't that honor!...

(DE LA PORCHERAIE *enters left.)*

LA PORCHERAIE: *(Holding a map, aside)* It's all set...I've managed to squeeze in five villas on the right and five on the left... Honestly, I don't know where they'll put their furniture... *(Aloud)* Mademoiselle Thérèse here? ...Has your school burned down?

THÉRÈSE: Oh! school...I'm never going back there again! ...My school days are over...I'm going to be married...

LA PORCHERAIE: Really! ...I won't ask to whom?... *(Aside)* Cousin to cousin...Dutrécy gets rid of them both at the same time!

FROMENTAL: But where is Dutrécy? ...Ah, here he comes!...

DUTRÉCY: *(Entering left)* Ah! Madame! ...Monsieur! ...A thousand pardons for keeping you waiting...but an urgent matter...

FROMENTAL. *(To* DUTRÉCY*)* My dear classmate...this is Georges, my son... A Saint-Barbian, like ourselves.

GEORGES: *(Bowing)* Monsieur Dutrécy...

DUTRÉCY: Delighted, Monsieur... *(Aside)* He looks all right!...

FROMENTAL: I have the honor of asking, on his behalf, the hand of Mademoiselle Thérèse, your niece...

ARMAND: *(Aside)* What? Him? *(He leans on a chair.)*

LA PORCHERAIE: Ah! Bah!...

MME DE VERRIÈRES: *(Aside, observing* ARMAND*)* That's peculiar! ...That young man...

DUTRÉCY. My dear Fromental...I never indulge in empty phrases...we are in too much of a hurry... It's a done deal...

ARMAND: *(Falling on to the chair)* Ah!...

MME DE VERRIÈRES: *(Watching him, aside)* He loves her!...

(Curtain)

END OF ACT ONE

ACT TWO

(At FROMENTAL's. *A drawing-room set up for an evening party.)*

*(*FROMENTAL, GEORGES *and* MME DE VERRIÈRES *are all dressed for a ball.* GEORGES *is sitting next to a table.)*

MME DE VERRIÈRES: *(In front of a mirror)* I'm ready to receive our guests.

FROMENTAL: So am I...

MME DE VERRIÈRES: Georges, what do you think of my outfit?

GEORGES: *(Not looking at her)* Charming!

MME DE VERRIÈRES: I wanted to be very pretty when I introduced my little sister-in-law to our friends... You're sad...what's the matter?

FROMENTAL: That's true... For two days now, ever since we asked for her hand, you haven't opened your mouth.

GEORGES: Nothing's the matter... Do you realize that I haven't seen Armand again...I've been to his home half a dozen times, and he hasn't paid me a single visit.

FROMENTAL: And that's why you're so down in the mouth? ...I could understand if it had to do with a classmate...a fellow alumnus...a...

GEORGES: Armand is more than that to me...he's a friend.

MME DE VERRIÈRES: Are you sure of that?

GEORGES: Oh yes! I can count on him...as I could on you! And by the way, father, I have a request...a favor to ask you...at some other time.

FROMENTAL: Why not now? Nobody's here yet! ... Speak, I'm listening.

GEORGES: Armand has no fortune...he has no position...and I would like to give him one...I owe it to him... Would you see any great difficulty in taking him into our firm?...

MME DE VERRIÈRES: What!

FROMENTAL: Ah, have you gone mad! You tell me has no capital!...

GEORGES: What about it?

FROMENTAL: What about it! See here, are we bankers, yes or no?

GEORGES: But, father...

FROMENTAL: After all, what is this Monsieur Armand you're so crazy about? ...An acquaintance you met on your travels! Suppose we were to make partners of all our travelling companions?

GEORGES: All right ! father, you are the master of what you possess; but you won't object if I turn over a portion of my share.

MME DE VERRIÈRES: (Aside) This is extraordinary...

FROMENTAL: This is sheer insanity, delirium... And what great service has Monsieur Armand done you?

GEORGES: Well, father, there is something I have concealed from you...I didn't want to tell you lest I increase your deep fear of travel... During my crossing, I fell ill with fever...severe fever...

MME DE VERRIÈRES: Good heavens!

FROMENTAL: Can it be?

GEORGES: The captain convened his officers…and he decided, on the spot, to land me on the first coastline they could reach.

MME DE VERRIÈRES: A sick man!

FROMENTAL: What! And you didn't protest! You didn't tell them, "I am the son of the Fromental Bank in Paris! We'll pay you, cowards though you are!"

GEORGES: I don't think that would have convinced them… Only one officer…a Frenchman, father! …Energetically stood up against this cowardly marooning…

FROMENTAL: That's fine!

GEORGES: He offered to share his cabin with me…but to no avail…I was barely conscious myself…I could feel two sailors carry me on a mattress and set me down in a canoe…soon the sound of oars told me that we had left the ship.

FROMENTAL: That's what comes of travelling!

GEORGES: A wave splashing over us made me open my eyes…and to my surprise I saw seated at the helm that same officer who had leapt to my defense, he grasped my hand and said, "*I* won't leave you!"

MME DE VERRIÈRES: Ah! that's wonderful!

FROMENTAL: A fine young man!

GEORGES: We landed.

FROMENTAL: And he immediately sent to the next town for a doctor!

GEORGES: There was no doctor, there was no next town… This was when his work of devotion and self-denial really began. For six weeks he sat at my bedside, he slept with his head on my bed, he fought the plague for me with the courage, the tenderness of a mother fighting for her child!

MME DE VERRIÈRES: Admirable!

FROMENTAL: Sublime!

GEORGES: Well, that friend…that brother…

FROMENTAL: Was Armand Bernier!

GEORGES: The very man!

MME DE VERRIÈRES: He! And he loves Thérèse!

FROMENTAL: Oh, but that's another story…a man who saved you…don't worry, we'll find him a position…an important position…

GEORGES: (Shaking his hand) I never doubted it!

A SERVANT: (Announcing) Monsieur Armand Bernier.

GEORGES: (Coming to him) Armand!

FROMENTAL: Come in, come in, my friend…my dear friend…we know everything!

MME DE VERRIÈRES: Monsieur Armand…I owe my brother to you…will you give me your hand?

ARMAND: (Giving her his hand) Madame…if I have won Georges's friendship…and a bit of your affection…I find myself only too well rewarded.

FROMENTAL: That may be reward enough in your eyes…but we like to pay our debts…in cash…

GEORGES: (Undertone) Father…

FROMENTAL: I need a cashier…I shall hire you…

ARMAND: If I may, Monsieur.

FROMENTAL: Salary eight thousand francs…and six per cent interest in the profits.

ARMAND: Thank you, Monsieur…but I could never tie myself down to office work.

FROMENTAL: Well, you can go about your business...I'll look after your duties...and Georges will help me!

GEORGES: Oh, with all my heart!

ARMAND: Really, I'm touched by your offer...but I am accustomed to sailing...I love the sea, and I have come to say good-bye, for I've leaving tomorrow for New York.

FROMENTAL & MME DE VERRIÈRES: What!

GEORGES: Leaving! That can't be! What about that marriage you mentioned?

ARMAND: No more thought is to be given to that marriage...it's broken off.

GEORGES: Ah, that's peculiar.

MME DE VERRIÈRES: *(Aside)* I understand...poor boy!

ARMAND: Georges, I entrust my little Thérèse to you... love her...the way a decent man should love his wife.

GEORGES: Oh, don't worry! ...Thérèse is my whole life!

ARMAND: Yes...I know...love me as well...I think I deserve it.

GEORGES: Why do you say that, Armand? ...There's something the matter...what have I done to you?

ARMAND: Never mind, my friend...it's nothing...

GEORGES: Oh, yes it is, we have to talk...you aren't the same man...I have to talk to you.

FROMENTAL: Do so! and stop him from leaving.

ARMAND: *(Bowing)* Madame...Monsieur... *(To* GEORGES, *as he exits.)* But I repeat it's nothing.

FROMENTAL: *(Aside)* There's something strange about that young man.

*(*GEORGES *and* ARMAND *exit.)*

MME DE VERRIÈRES: *(Aside)* Such a sacrifice… Oh no! Georges would never accept it! *(Aloud)* Father, Monsieur Armand loves Thérèse…

FROMENTAL: Good heavens! What are you saying?

MME DE VERRIÈRES: I say that you have to let Georges know.

FROMENTAL: Really!

MME DE VERRIÈRES: He would be too unhappy if he stole Thérèse's hand from the man who saved him!

FROMENTAL: Come, come! Don't get excited! Don't get overwrought and especially don't say anything to Georges…he'd be just as liable to fly off the handle as you are… First of all you may be mistaken!…

MME DE VERRIÈRES: No, father.

FROMENTAL: Then it's unfortunate…but we can do nothing about it.

MME DE VERRIÈRES: You could speak…

FROMENTAL: A marriage announced all over the place…a charming young bride…whom your brother adores.

MME DE VERRIÈRES: But if Georges were to give her up on his own?

FROMENTAL: But since we've agreed not to speak of it to Georges.

MME DE VERRIÈRES: Then you condemn him to be an ingrate.

FROMENTAL: Ingrate! Ingrate!

SERVANT: *(Announcing)* Monsieur de la Porcheraie!

FROMENTAL: We shall resume this discussion…but not a word to Georges.

(DE LA PORCHERAIE enters. FROMENTAL goes to meet him.)

FROMENTAL: Good evening, my dear friend...

LA PORCHERAIE: (*Gives his hand to* FROMENTAL *and bows to* MME DE VERRIÈRES) Madame... Are you expecting the doctor this evening?

FROMENTAL: Yes...we hope to see him.

LA PORCHERAIE: He is a slippery character...I arranged to meet him at my place...he never showed up...so I went to his place...nobody there!

FROMENTAL: Are you ill?

LA PORCHERAIE: Eh!...

MME DE VERRIÈRES: Then, Monsieur, we have doubly to thank you for putting aside your indisposition to come to our little party.

LA PORCHERAIE: Don't mention it, Madame...but there are pleasures for which one would brave anything... (*Aside*) They're stuck on themselves! ...If I didn't have to see the doctor, I would have stayed at my club...I was winning.

SERVANT: (*Announcing*) Monsieur and Madame de Puysole.

(*Several guests appear.* FROMENTAL *and* MME DE VERRIÈRES *go upstage to greet them.*)

FROMENTAL: (*Greeting a lady*) Madame... (*Giving his hand to a little schoolboy wearing the Sainte-Barbe uniform.*) My dear classmate from Saint-Barbe...

LA PORCHERAIE: (*Aside*) All Barbarians here!

(FROMENTAL *and* MME DE VERRIÈRES *go into the drawing-rooms with the guests.*)

SERVANT: (*Announcing*) Doctor Fourcinier.

LA PORCHERAIE: (*Aside*) Ah! here's my man!

(*Stopping* FOURCINIER *who is about to enter the drawing-room:*)

LA PORCHERAIE: Sorry! Sorry! I need a consultation.

FOURCINIER: Ah, it's you!

LA PORCHERAIE: Doctor, you abandoned me...I waited for you on Wednesday at four o'clock.

FOURCINIER: Ah, my friend...it was impossible to visit you... The fact is, I have a garden in Passy...

LA PORCHERAIE: (Aside) Good! He's getting down to it!

FOURCINIER: A very big garden...

LA PORCHERAIE: Yes, I know...

FOURCINIER: And there's a rumor that they're going to build a slaughter-house just across from my front gate.

LA PORCHERAIE: I have heard something about it...it's a sure thing!

FOURCINIER: No! it's a lie! ...Today I went to City Hall...it's never even been suggested.

LA PORCHERAIE: Ah! (Aside) One misfire! (Aloud) By the way, what are you planning to do with that garden?

FOURCINIER: Well! I am going to stroll in it on Sundays... Do you know it?

LA PORCHERAIE: Yes...I stepped inside once...by accident...it's ugly!

FOURCINIER: There's a cedar of Lebanon on the lawn!

LA PORCHERAIE: What can a cedar of Lebanon bring in...year in, year out?

FOURCINIER: Oh! this isn't a commercial property... it's a pleasure garden... And, between you and me, something's going on...Wednesday morning a gentleman came with a surveyor who had laid out a map of the garden.

LA PORCHERAIE: (Aside) That was me! Happy thought!

FOURCINIER: Evidently someone has plans.

LA PORCHERAIE: No…it's the government land-survey!

FOURCINIER: What land-survey?

LA PORCHERAIE: Yes, in order to readjust the taxes…
Everyone will get an increase!

FOURCINIER: The devil you say! I pay plenty already…
for a garden that doesn't bring in anything…

LA PORCHERAIE: Except apricots…and this isn't a good
year for them! Well, I'll buy your garden from you.

FOURCINIER: You? You must be joking!

LA PORCHERAIE: Seriously…

FOURCINIER: Ah!

LA PORCHERAIE: I shall arrange it to my taste and I'll
spend the summers there. How much are you willing
to sell it for?

FOURCINIER: But…I don't want to sell it.

LA PORCHERAIE: Naturally! since I've shown an
interest.

FOURCINIER: No… The property reminds me of the
past…I played there when I was a child…my father
lived in the cottage.

LA PORCHERAIE: That shack?

FOURCINIER: Shack!

LA PORCHERAIE: It can't stand up… You mustn't cough
too close to the retaining wall! Come now…will you
take a hundred thousand francs?

FOURCINIER: It was in that little white cottage…with the
green shutters…that I wed my wife…

LA PORCHERAIE: (Aside) Uh-oh! sentiment! It's getting
expensive!

FOURCINIER: It was there…only later…I had the
misfortune to lose her…

LA PORCHERAIE: You see…your property makes you sad…constantly to have before your eyes the place where she was struck down! …A hundred and fifteen!

FOURCINIER: No! I cherish my grief! I suffer a cruel… but sweet pleasure in sitting beneath the tree where we spent such long evenings.

LA PORCHERAIE: *(Aside)* He's a tough nut! *(Aloud)* A hundred and thirty!

FOURCINIER: It's not enough…

LA PORCHERAIE: What!

FOURCINIER: It's not enough to have loved one's wife… one must still know how to preserve a little plot of earth replete with her memory.

LA PORCHERAIE: Keep it then! …I won't say another word about it.

FOURCINIER: *(Disappointed)* Ah! Just as well! I might perhaps have ended up being tempted.

LA PORCHERAIE: Your grief is highly respectable…but it's a bottomless pit…I might perhaps have gone as high as a hundred and fifty thousand francs.

FOURCINIER: Say what?…

LA PORCHERAIE: A hundred and fifty thousand.

FOURCINIER: Without the furniture?

LA PORCHERAIE: I can just picture your furniture! Six rickety armchairs and a piano with snapping strings…

FOURCINIER: They are memories…

LA PORCHERAIE: Yes, you want to sell them retail.

FOURCINIER: Never!…

LA PORCHERAIE: I'll let you keep your furniture! …A hundred and fifty thousand…agreed.

FOURCINIER: Only...I'd like till tomorrow morning to sleep on it.

LA PORCHERAIE: All right, I'll be at your place at ten o'clock!

FOURCINIER: Ten o'clock! I shall be waiting! ...Oh yes! our consultation...what's the matter with you?

LA PORCHERAIE: Practically nothing...I can no longer digest crayfish.

FOURCINIER: Then you mustn't eat them.

LA PORCHERAIE: Thanks...I thought so!

SERVANT: *(Announcing)* Monsieur and Madame Dutrécy.

(DUTRÉCY and THÉRÈSE enter. He is dressed elegantly with a youthful turned-down collar.)

LA PORCHERAIE: What, Madame Dutrécy... Thérèse!

DUTRÉCY: It's a mistake...but no harm done... Good evening, Doctor!

FOURCINIER: *(Bowing)* My dear friend... Mademoiselle!...

DUTRÉCY: *(To THÉRÈSE)* Well, my dear child! Here we are at the ball! Are you pleased?

THÉRÈSE: Yes, uncle!

DUTRÉCY: You're not too warm?

THÉRÈSE: No, uncle.

DUTRÉCY: You're not too cold?

THÉRÈSE: No, uncle.

DUTRÉCY: You should have kept your fur wrap... Would you like me to fetch it for you?

THÉRÈSE: There's no point.

DUTRÉCY: *(Undertone to* DE LA PORCHERAIE*)* Isn't she pretty in her ball gown?

LA PORCHERAIE: *(Aside, astonished)* What's come over him?... *(Undertone to* DUTRÉCY*)* I've almost clinched the deal with Fourcinier...I have to talk to you.

DUTRÉCY: *(Looking at* THÉRÈSE*)* Yes...tomorrow...

LA PORCHERAIE: No! right now!

DUTRÉCY: Doctor! would you be so kind as to escort Thérèse to Madame de Verrières.

FOURCINIER: But of course! *(Offering his arm)* Mademoiselle.

DUTRÉCY: *(To* THÉRÈSE*)* In five minutes...I shall join you...don't be impatient! Doctor, I entrust her to you!

*(*FOURCINIER *and* THÉRÈSE *exit.)*

LA PORCHERAIE: I've just settled with Fourcinier for a hundred and fifty thousand...it's a done deal, in other words...he asked me to hold off till tomorrow morning.

DUTRÉCY: *(Distracted, looking through the drawing-room door)* That's good! All the better, I'm quite content...

LA PORCHERAIE: What's the matter with you? ...You're not listening to me...

DUTRÉCY: Of course I am...but Thérèse is all by herself in there...

LA PORCHERAIE: So what! Are you supposed to be playing chaperone?

DUTRÉCY: My friend... That young lady...is an angel! The more I know her, the more I appreciate her.

LA PORCHERAIE: Indeed!

DUTRÉCY: I fully expected to see her ensconced in my house for two weeks...I was thinking...my whole way of life will be upset, overturned... Well! not at all! you

barely hear a peep out of her... She trips about the
apartment like a little bird... If I need her...there she is,
when I want to be alone...she flies away.

LA PORCHERAIE: *(Aside)* And he's turned down his
collar!

DUTRÉCY: It's very pleasant to have a companion...
who doesn't bother you... You know I don't like to eat
alone...Forcinier has forbidden it... Well! she keeps me
company...she does the carving...she's very nimble...
she talks, she chatters, she prattles...she tells me about
her life at school. I already know the names of her little
classmates...with their faults!

LA PORCHERAIE: Much good that'll do you!

DUTRÉCY: Ah, it's charming!

LA PORCHERAIE: Papa Dutrécy...we are in love!

DUTRÉCY: Me? Hush! *(Confidentially)* I am afraid I
might be. Just now, when that servant announced
Monsieur and Madame Dutrécy...I felt my face go
red...and I liked it!

LA PORCHERAIE: Really?

DUTRÉCY: Which proves that it wouldn't be so
ridiculous...

LA PORCHERAIE: Come, come... Isn't she too young for
you?

DUTRÉCY: You don't know her... She is young when
she has to be...and sensible, staid, when need be.

LA PORCHERAIE: And how did you catch this disease?

DUTRÉCY: I have no idea...watching her organize the
closets...she arranged my linen, my suits. Ah! how
nicely such a woman takes care of a person! Last night
she heard me cough and personally brewed a little
violet tea with honey...like at school, and I stopped
coughing.

LA PORCHERAIE: You don't say so!

DUTRÉCY: She kept me company all night along…she read me the latest best-seller…and her diction! …You can hear all the words… You should see her laugh… dainty teeth…like pearls…

LA PORCHERAIE: Watch out! …Pearls require society to set them off…glittering lights.

DUTRÉCY: Oh! not Thérèse, she's a homebody; she spends the evening doing embroidery.

LA PORCHERAIE: Yes, they're all like that…until they get married…but afterward! …I've been caught myself!

DUTRÉCY: You, how was that?

LA PORCHERAIE: And what about my wife?

DUTRÉCY: What! you're married?

LA PORCHERAIE: Of course I am! Didn't you know?

DUTRÉCY: No!

LA PORCHERAIE: I thought you knew.

DUTRÉCY: I've known you for ten years and this is the first time…you never introduced me to the lady…

LA PORCHERAIE: Oh really! as if I knew where the hell she is! It'll soon be eleven years since we lost sight of one another.

DUTRÉCY: Separated?

LA PORCHERAIE: We stayed together for seven or eight months…I'm not exactly sure. She was a very respectable woman…but impossible to live with! A social butterfly! All she dreamed about were parties and pleasures! Every day she would drag me to a ball or a concert…in unhealthy places…airless…outside the theatre we would have to wait for our carriage…I would catch cold and the next day…do you think she was resting? Not at all! She would sit down at her piano...at dawn, she would hammer out polkas, waltzes. It was unbearable! Finally, one day I said to her: Madame, take your fortune, I'll take mine, and do me the kindness of dancing somewhere else!

DUTRÉCY: I can understand that... And you never saw her again?

LA PORCHERAIE: Yes, once...on the train to Mulhouse.

DUTRÉCY: Ah!

LA PORCHERAIE: We bowed! ...I sometimes inquire after her and she sends me a New Year's card...we're not on bad terms.

DUTRÉCY: Oh, but I! with Thérèse...I don't have to fear such an ending...she doesn't care for balls... She is used to going to bed at an early hour...she's a little sleepyhead... At school, we used to call her... (Catching himself) they used to call her...Mademoiselle Dormouse!

LA PORCHERAIE: Exquisite temperament! Oh! a woman who sleeps!

DUTRÉCY: Now, my friend, tell me frankly...don't flatter me...I'm fifty-four...

LA PORCHERAIE: Oh!

DUTRÉCY: Not much more...I am admirably preserved. Would you advise me to marry Thérèse?

LA PORCHERAIE: In the first instance, would she have you?

DUTRÉCY: I'm richer than she is!

LA PORCHERAIE: And what if she loves Georges, her fiancé?

DUTRÉCY: Oh, no, she's not in love with the fiancé, but with the idea of marriage.

LA PORCHERAIE: Then, here's my opinion. In this world you should do whatever promises to give you satisfaction… Let's work this out…you are in love?

DUTRÉCY: *(Cautiously)* I think so.

LA PORCHERAIE: Therefore, you would be happy living with Thérèse… If later on she gets tired of you, if she cheats on you…

DUTRÉCY: What!

LA PORCHERAIE: You wouldn't know! and you would be only the better cared for… Therefore, it's a good match in either case, so get married!

DUTRÉCY: You have such a way of putting things…

LA PORCHERAIE: And then, marriage, they say, provides a comfort zone; it's an orange tree under which you set a bench where you can rest…I don't see any drawback in sitting there…if it doesn't suit you, you can do as I did and get up!

DUTRÉCY: I'm not going to get married just to sit down!

LA PORCHERAIE: Now, as to what concerns me…if your house becomes less agreeable…if your wife imposes discomforts and constraints on me…I shall never visit you again, and that's that!

DUTRÉCY: That's that! There is something which bothers me a little.

LA PORCHERAIE: What's that?

DUTRÉCY: I gave my word to Georges…

LA PORCHERAIE: You can take it back… Find a pretext!

DUTRÉCY: I've looked; but it isn't easy…I have to persuade him to give her up on his own.

LA PORCHERAIE: Well! use Armand to trip him up.

DUTRÉCY: Armand?

LA PORCHERAIE: He loves Thérèse too.

DUTRÉCY: He does! Impossible!

LA PORCHERAIE: There are three of you. A number pleasing to the gods. What! you never had an inkling of a lover!

DUTRÉCY: Good Lord! That's a lucky discovery! Armand saved Georges...

LA PORCHERAIE: He carried his tree!

DUTRÉCY: That's true! And if the other fellow has even a bit of heart...

LA PORCHERAIE: Oh, don't count on that! ...In love, the heart is given whole... There's nothing left for the bystanders.

DUTRÉCY: Oh! Georges is one of the better natures!

LA PORCHERAIE: Well, anyway...try it! I'm off.

DUTRÉCY: You're going?

LA PORCHERAIE: This family reunion is not wildly exciting...I'm going to smoke a cigar at my club... Good-bye...young man!... *(He exits.)*

DUTRÉCY: *(Alone)* It will be very difficult for Georges to sacrifice himself in turn. If I were in his shoes...and I were his age! ...Here he is!

GEORGES: *(Entering; aside)* Impossible to pry a word out of Armand! Monsieur Dutrècy...alone... What are you doing here?

DUTRÉCY: My friend...it's more than I can deal with... this ball...this music...when one has a secret sorrow...

GEORGES: You?...

DUTRÉCY: I have just heard a piece of news which devastates me. You know how fond I am of Armand?

GEORGES: He is sad...unhappy...

DUTRÉCY: Ah! you've noticed it?

GEORGES: Right away! But the cause of his sorrow, do you know it?

DUTRÉCY: Yes… just imagine…but no, I can't tell you… you are the last person…

GEORGES: Oh, speak! There is a…boundless affection between Armand and me! My life is his!

DUTRÉCY: *(Taking him by the hand)* Georges! You have a noble heart! *(Aside)* It'll work! *(Aloud)* Then learn…I was far from expecting…learn that Armand is love with his cousin Thérèse!

GEORGES: *(Dumbfounded)* Armand! Impossible! Since when?

DUTRÉCY: A childhood romance…secret, but intense! He hoped to marry her on his return from America… You showed up ahead of him…and there we are!

GEORGES: Ah! I have no happiness! *(He sits next to the table and puts his head in his hands.)*

DUTRÉCY: *(Aside)* He's going to retract his proposal. *(Aloud)* After all, *you* can't do anything about it… Armand is young…he'll get over it!…

GEORGES: *(Quickly)* Ah, you think he'll get over it?

DUTRÉCY: What I mean is…I really don't know! You mustn't take what I say literally… *(Aside)* I shouldn't have said that. *(Aloud)* He might die of it!

GEORGES: *(To himself, not listening to* DUTRÉCY*)* Thérèse, Thérèse!

DUTRÉCY: Good old Armand! Now there's a fellow who knows how to love his friends… He doesn't hesitate! I'm told he was very good to you on the voyage?

(DUTRÉCY *awaits an answer from* GEORGES *who remains silent, his head in his hands.*)

DUTRÉCY: What's he doing? ...Is he asleep? (*Coughing.*) Ahem. (*Aloud*) I'm told he was very good to you on the voyage?

GEORGES: Perfectly! Monsieur, perfectly!

DUTRÉCY: Yes, perfectly... (*Aside*) He's cold... (*Aloud*) What answer shall I bring the poor boy?

GEORGES: Eh! Monsieur! Spare me...give me some time...when you have to tear your heart out with your own hands...

DUTRÉCY: Quite right! take your time. (*Aside, as he exits.*) He's a bit self-involved, this little young man... but he'll get there! ...Armand! ...Let's leave them together! (*He exits.*)

ARMAND: (*Entering*) My friend...

GEORGES: Armand!

ARMAND: I've been looking for you...I wanted to ask your permission to withdraw! ...Were you kind enough to write those letters of recommendation I asked you for New York?...

GEORGES: No...I kept hoping that you wouldn't leave.

ARMAND: My departure is urgent...indispensable.

GEORGES: Armand!

ARMAND: What?

GEORGES: You'll write, won't you?

ARMAND: Oh, all the time! And you'll answer me, you'll send me news of yourself...and Thérèse... (*With effort*) your wife...

GEORGES: Oh! if you only knew how much pain I'm in!

ARMAND: Actually...you are pale...

GEORGES: I'm struggling…I'm contending…with a sorrow…

ARMAND: A sorrow? What sort?

GEORGES: *(Quickly)* At your departure… On the other hand…I understand…because… Good-bye! …I'm going to write those letters… *(Aside)* Oh! I can't, I love her too much! *(He goes off right.)*

ARMAND: *(Alone)* That tormented expression…those incoherent words… Can I have given myself away! … Oh no! I know Georges; if he had the least suspicion, he wouldn't have gone to write those letters!

DUTRÉCY: *(Entering)* It makes no sense! They open a window just when Thérèse is starting to waltz! I'll fetch her fur wrap.

ARMAND: Uncle!

DUTRÉCY: Ah! it's you, my friend! …Well, have you seen Georges?

ARMAND: He just left me.

DUTRÉCY: Well?

ARMAND: What?

DUTRÉCY: Did he say anything?

ARMAND: No…what was he supposed to say?

DUTRÉCY: This is amazing! After all, what do you expect, my poor fellow! It's not my fault…you spoke too late!

ARMAND: *I* did?

DUTRÉCY: It was the dream of my life! …Two children whom I had raised!

ARMAND: What are you talking about?

DUTRÉCY: Thérèse, your beloved!

ARMAND: *(Quickly)* Oh, keep still, what if Georges were to hear you!

DUTRÉCY: He knows all about it, I told him...

ARMAND: What! you told Georges that I loved Thérèse?

DUTRÉCY: Absolutely!

ARMAND: And what was his reaction?

DUTRÉCY: Nothing!

ARMAND: Ah!...

DUTRÉCY: Ah! ...He pretended to be asleep.

ARMAND: Oh, that can't be!

DUTRÉCY: His is a soul without sublimity...after all you've done for him.

ARMAND: Oh, let's not talk about that!

DUTRÉCY: On the contrary, let's! I believe that if you were to utter a few forceful words to him! if you were to say, "Georges, I carried your tree, you carry mine"!

ARMAND: What's the use?

DUTRÉCY: Why, it would break everything off...and I could...and you could marry Thérèse...it's worth thinking about! ...Where's the cloakroom? Ah! I say it's worth thinking about!... *(Aside)* I'm quite pleased with myself! *(He exits.)*

ARMAND: *(Alone)* No, I won't say a word to him!

(Noticing GEORGES enter:)

ARMAND: There he is!

GEORGES: *(Enters holding letters; he is very pale and upset)* Here are the letters you asked for... There are two...I wanted to write a lot of them...but tonight...my hand is trembling. One is for our branch in New York; I asked them to open a credit account for you...

ARMAND: That's good of you!

GEORGES: The other is addressed to Messrs Anderson and Blum, two ship-owners who, at my suggestion...

ARMAND: Thank you!

GEORGES: (*Approaches* ARMAND *and suddenly tears up the two letters*) No, you shall not leave, it's out of the question!

ARMAND: Ah!

(ARMAND *and* GEORGES *throw themselves into one another's arms.*)

GEORGES: You love Thérèse...marry her...take her away! But I shall never see her again!

ARMAND: (*Holding out his arms*) Ah! Georges!

GEORGES: (*Rushing into them*) My friend, my friend, forgive me for having hesitated... But I loved her so much!

ARMAND: Dear boy! I will not accept your sacrifice...I desired it...I expected it...but I do not choose to accept it... Well now, uncle! ...And you, Monsieur de la Porcheraie, there still people on this earth who love and are devoted to one another: Dear Georges! I shall leave in peace...for I am sure now that Thérèse is marrying a brave heart!

GEORGES: Oh! be still! Don't tempt me...I shall grow weak again... cowardly...

ARMAND: Georges!

GEORGES: No! I know what I have to do! (*He exits quickly.*)

ARMAND: (*Alone*) Where are you going? ...Ah! do whatever you want...tomorrow I shall be gone.

(*Noticing* THÉRÈSE *enter.*)

ARMAND: Thérèse! Oh! my heart! No, I don't want to see her! (*He heads for the door at back.*)

THÉRÈSE: Well, cousin, people run away when I come in!

ARMAND: Sorry…I didn't see you…

THÉRÈSE: I've been looking for you all over the ballroom for the last hour.

ARMAND: *(Coming close to her)* Really! you were thinking about me?

THÉRÈSE: I should say so… It's your turn now…

ARMAND: Turn?

THÉRÈSE: I put you down on my dance card for the eighth quadrille…

ARMAND: Ah, that's the reason…I beg your pardon… but this evening…I'm not in the mood…

THÉRÈSE: What! you don't want to dance.

ARMAND: Excuse me…

THÉRÈSE: You should have told me! …I turned down three invitations… Now you've made me miss the quadrille…I'm going back to my seat. *(About to exit.)*

ARMAND: *(Holding her back)* Stay here…please… Since you were willing to grant me a quadrille…let's use the time…to talk…will you?

THÉRÈSE: It's not the same thing.

ARMAND: *(Gesturing for her to sit)* Thérèse…

THÉRÈSE: *(Aside)* He's a bore.

ARMAND: I've hardly seen you since I've been back… do you have anything to say to me?

THÉRÈSE: People don't go to balls to talk…I think we chatted enough this morning…and I don't see… Ah yes, a meeting…you know Lucie…

ARMAND: Lucie…no!

THÉRÈSE: Yes you do…you saw her in the drawing-room…she's a married lady.

ARMAND: Ah!

THÉRÈSE: Last year she took the waters at Aix with seventeen frocks; what a happy lady!

ARMAND: Ah yes! so anyone who travels with eighteen frocks would be even happier?

THÉRÈSE: That's not what I mean.

(The music can be heard at one side.)

THÉRÈSE: Do you hear the orchestra…they're starting…

ARMAND: Go on, I'd feel guilty for keeping you any longer.

THÉRÈSE: Oh, it's too late now… everyone's in place… All right, what do you have to say to me?

ARMAND: Oh! nothing very interesting…I wanted to talk to you about your memories…of our friendship as children…we were separated…but what happiness when we could be together again…when my uncle would take me into the reception room of your school…how my heart was pounding!

THÉRÈSE: Oh, mine too!

ARMAND: Really?

THÉRÈSE: You always brought me a bag of candied chestnuts.

ARMAND: Ah!

THÉRÈSE: It was very kind of you to think of me that way…

ARMAND: I had saved up for a month from my pitiful allowance.

THÉRÈSE: I especially liked the vanilla ones.

ARMAND: Unfortunately! Those cost two francs more than the others.

THÉRÈSE: Poor Armand! Weren't you sweet! *(Laughing)* But you did look funny in your school uniform...which was too short.

ARMAND: Eh?

THÉRÈSE: Ah, you did make us young ladies laugh! The older ones drew your caricature...I thought that was mean!

ARMAND: Thérèse! Is this really you? You so serious... so kind-hearted...who always walked with her eyes on the ground.

THÉRÈSE: That...our deportment teacher suggested it to me.

ARMAND: What! those long, soulful looks?...

THÉRÈSE: Ah! I had a lot of trouble getting those down pat! But the teacher always said to me; "Mademoiselle Thérèse, you laugh too much! It isn't respectable— think of something sad!"

ARMAND: And what did you think about?

THÉRÈSE: I'd think that Booboo, our little school cat, was dying! ...What's the matter?...

ARMAND: Nothing... *(Aside)* Booboo!... *(Aloud)* Go on! ...I need all my strength...I need to hear you! ...So, I looked ridiculous to you?

THÉRÈSE: Oh, I didn't say that!

ARMAND: With my clothes too short...

THÉRÈSE: *(Laughing)* And your big shoes...always untied.

ARMAND: And you never noticed anything else?

THÉRÈSE: No! ...Why do you ask?

ARMAND: Oh, no reason… *(Aside)* Oh! my dreams! My dreams!

THÉRÈSE: Armand… Are you in pain?

ARMAND: Pay it no mind…I'm getting over my fever… it's on its way out…it's gone! Ah! I feel much better!

THÉRÈSE: Would you like me to call our uncle?

ARMAND: No need… *(Taking her by the hand)* See, my hand clasps yours and doesn't tremble…my gaze is steady…Thérèse, I can dance with you now…I have no more fears…

THÉRÈSE: Ah, so sorry! but that round is over! I am engaged for the ninth…

ARMAND: Quite right!

THÉRÈSE: That'll teach you to waste your time…

ARMAND: Oh! I don't mind! *(Holding out his hand to her)* Good-bye!

THÉRÈSE: So long!

ARMAND: *(Scrutinizing her)* Isn't that peculiar! I always thought you had blue eyes!

THÉRÈSE: Well?

ARMAND: They're gray!

THÉRÈSE: *(Pulling her hand away)* Huh! I must confess, Monsieur, that you are not very likeable at balls…I won't hold it against you! *(She exits.)*

ARMAND: Go quickly, you're going to miss the quadrille! *(Alone)* Ah! my heart is free again…I can breathe…and good old Georges!…

(MME DE VERRIÈRES enters.)

ARMAND: Madame…

MME DE VERRIÈRES: Monsieur Armand!

ARMAND: Ah! Madame, if you knew how happy I am!
I've just seen Thérèse!

MME DE VERRIÈRES: And I have just left my brother...
Poor boy! it pains me to see...but he will behave
chivalrously...

ARMAND: He will marry Thérèse and I shall be his best
man! and I shall dance at his wedding!

MME DE VERRIÈRES: Ah, my goodness! ...Monsieur...
come to your senses!...

ARMAND: Which is what I have done, Madame...my
senses are restored...

MME DE VERRIÈRES: How?

ARMAND: During the eighth quadrille.

MME DE VERRIÈRES: I don't understand...

ARMAND: I spoke with Thérèse...she's an angel! She
shares none of my tastes! ...She loves society, balls,
frocks, the school cat, Booboo... Five minutes were
enough to demolish my romance from top to bottom.

MME DE VERRIÈRES: What! you don't love her any
longer?

ARMAND: I never loved her...it was somebody else...it
was a fantasy Thérèse that I loved...sailors are used to
those sorts of mirages... Have you sailed, Madame?...

MME DE VERRIÈRES: Very little!

ARMAND: How many times it happened that I would
fall in love at a distance with one of those pretty little
towns that spring up among the rocks on the beach...
A ray of moonlight...a passing mood makes them seem
gentle, quiet, melancholy... You think you'd like to end
your days there in the calm and silence of the heart...
You come closer, you land...this town is full of fiddles,
laughter and drums! So you get back on board as fast

as you can, and set off in search of a new ideal...that you may never encounter.

MME DE VERRIÈRES: Why so? You mustn't despair.

ARMAND: No, you see, I'm looking for the impossible... I'm looking for a woman who never flirts...

MME DE VERRIÈRES: *(Aside)* How chivalrous!

ARMAND: But let's not talk about me...let's talk about Georges.

MME DE VERRIÈRES: My poor brother...how happy he'll be...when I tell him he may love Thérèse without fear...without remorse...

ARMAND: The dear fellow...if you had witnessed his courage...I turned down his sacrifice, but with what joy I saw his devotion!

MME DE VERRIÈRES: Ah, what a friend you are!

FROMENTAL: *(Entering with* FOURCINIER*)* What, Doctor, leaving us already?

FOURCINIER: I have to!

FROMENTAL: By the way, you have a garden in Passy?

FOURCINIER: I do!

FROMENTAL: What are you doing with it?

FOURCINIER: Why...I walk around... *(Aside)* Why in the world do they all talk to me about my garden?

GEORGES: *(Entering; aside)* Monsieur Dutrécy is not to be found...

ARMAND: Georges!...

GEORGES: My friend...

ARMAND: Run quick and rewrite those letters of recommendation you tore up!

GEORGES: What?

ARMAND: My departure is set! Nothing can stop me.

GEORGES: All right. Count on me. *(Aside)* A thunderclap is the only way.

DUTRÉCY: *(Entering with a fur wrap)* Here it is, I lost the coat-check!

GEORGES: *(Aside)* Monsieur Dutrécy, can you grant me a word?

DUTRÉCY: I'm all yours, young man.

GEORGES: I have come to ask you to cancel our agreement.

EVERYONE: What!

ARMAND: *(To GEORGES)* Wretched man! What are you doing?

DUTRÉCY: Monsieur...such an insult to me and my family!

ARMAND: But, uncle...

DUTRÉCY: Armand, I forbid you to fight!

ARMAND: I didn't intend to! But...

DUTRÉCY: Not another word!

FROMENTAL: My dear classmate.

DUTRÉCY: *(Noticing THÉRÈSE)* Thérèse! ...Ah, gentlemen, let us be mindful of this child's sensitivity.

THÉRÈSE: What's going on?

DUTRÉCY: Nothing... *(Embracing THÉRÈSE)* You still have your uncle. *(Movement from THÉRÈSE)* Let us be gone! ...Let us quit this house forever.

EVERYONE: Monsieur Dutrécy!

DUTRÉCY: I am deaf to entreaties...I am outraged...I am... Watch out for drafts...

MME DE VERRIÈRES: *(Undertone to* ARMAND*)* Stay!…I have to talk to you!

(Curtain)

END OF ACT TWO

ACT THREE

(DUTRÉCY's *house. Same setting as ACT ONE*)

(DUTRÉCY *and* THÉRÈSE *are having lunch.* AUBIN *is serving them.*)

AUBIN: *(Aside, downstage)* I don't know how to tell the master...I've found another job...a hundred francs more and nothing to rub down.

THÉRÈSE: *(Aside)* Armand hasn't come back...Uncle, why did you put lunch forward half an hour?

DUTRÉCY: I don't know...this morning, after my shower, I felt I had an appetite...

THÉRÈSE: But cousin Armand won't get here till we've finished...

DUTRÉCY: *(Aside)* I hope so...that nephew is a nuisance. *(Aloud)* Does it bore you to have lunch alone with me?

THÉRÈSE: Oh, really! On the contrary I'm glad to be with you.

DUTRÉCY: Honestly?

THÉRÈSE: *(Aside)* I'm awfully worried he'll send me back to Mademoiselle Pinta! *(Aloud)* I'll carve the fowl!

DUTRÉCY: No, leave it...I'll call Cyprien.

THÉRÈSE: Oh, I so much enjoy fussing over you!...

DUTRÉCY: Precious girl! *(Watching her carve. Aside)* Those little hands are so nimble…as if she were snipping out a bit of embroidery.

THÉRÈSE: There! …There's a wing!

DUTRÉCY: Take the other one!

THÉRÈSE: Oh no!…

DUTRÉCY: Why not?

THÉRÈSE: In case you want to eat both of them…

DUTRÉCY: *(Aside, in ecstasy)* She thinks of everything! She's an angel! *(Calling.)* Aubin!

AUBIN: *(Drawing near)* Monsieur!

DUTRÉCY: *(In an undertone)* Give her the red seal!

AUBIN: Yes, Monsieur… *(He puts the bottle with the green seal under his arm and pours red seal for* THÉRÈSE.*)*

DUTRÉCY: *(To* THÉRÈSE*)* Just taste that…

THÉRÈSE: Wait. *(She pours water into it.)*

DUTRÉCY: Oh no! …Not water!…

THÉRÈSE: I don't like undiluted wine!… *(After drinking it.)* It's still too strong! *(She picks up the carafe and pours in more water.)*

DUTRÉCY: Aubin!

AUBIN: Monsieur.

DUTRÉCY: *(Undertone)* I've changed my mind…since she puts water in it, you will give her the green seal from now on.

AUBIN: Yes, Monsieur. *(Aside)* Now's the time to turn in my notice…Monsieur…

DUTRÉCY: *(To* THÉRÈSE*)* Shortly we'll take the buggy… and go together to the Bois.

THÉRÈSE: Is it going to rain?

DUTRÉCY: No, but you have to go out, have some distractions...we'll drive down a deserted lane...

AUBIN: Monsieur...

DUTRÉCY: What?

AUBIN: I have some information for Monsieur.

DUTRÉCY: All right...later!

AUBIN: It's just that...

DUTRÉCY: Leave us alone! Get out!

THÉRÈSE: Go on! ...I can serve the coffee myself. *(She gets up.)*

AUBIN: *(Exiting; aside)* Still I've got to let them know. *(He disappears.)*

DUTRÉCY: It's insufferable always having that big scarecrow behind your back!

THÉRÈSE: *(Bringing the coffee)* Here's your coffee... don't move! ...I'll pour it out for you... *(She pours.)* It's boiling hot... Now the sugar... *(She fetches the sugar bowl from the dresser.)* How many lumps?

DUTRÉCY: Three.

THÉRÈSE: One, two, three! And this little one into the bargain.

DUTRÉCY: *(Aside; blissfully lying back in his armchair)* This is it...this is true happiness! ...You forgot the brandy.

THÉRÈSE: On purpose. It's no good for you.

DUTRÉCY: You don't want me to have it?

THÉRÈSE: No!

DUTRÉCY: All right! I won't have it! *(Aside)* This child will have me live an extra ten years!

THÉRÈSE: *(Aside)* He's in a good mood... Do I dare mention Georges...

DUTRÉCY: *(Savoring his cup of coffee)* I've never had better coffee!… *(Aside)* Afterwards, I'll have her read the paper to me.

THÉRÈSE: Uncle…

DUTRÉCY: My child?…

THÉRÈSE: Isn't it incredible what that young man did yesterday?…

DUTRÉCY: What young man?

THÉRÈSE: You know very well…Monsieur Georges!

DUTRÉCY: He's a little fool! …To refuse your hand!

THÉRÈSE: That's it, uncle, it doesn't seem possible! You must surely have misheard…and if I had been there…

DUTRÉCY: There's nothing wrong with my ears!

THÉRÈSE: But what cause?

DUTRÉCY: Who knows? …Maybe he has another loved one in mind?

THÉRÈSE: Oh, I'm sure that's not the case!…

DUTRÉCY: You see, with young men you can't count on anything…a man's mind becomes really settled only at the age of fifty to fifty-four.

THÉRÈSE: *(Naively)* Much good it'll do at that age…

DUTRÉCY: But don't worry…we shall find you another husband…

THÉRÈSE: Another!…

DUTRÉCY: Well, goodness me! …He can't be as far away as you may think…and, meanwhile, we shall keep house together. *(He kisses her hand.)*

THÉRÈSE: So I won't be going back to Mademoiselle Pinta?

DUTRÉCY: Never!

THÉRÈSE: Honest to goodness! Honest to goodness!

DUTRÉCY: I swear it!

THÉRÈSE: Ah! I'm so happy! *(Aside)* I can see Georges again!

DUTRÉCY: *(Aside)* I think she's growing attached to me! *(Aloud)* Where's my newspaper?

THÉRÈSE: *(Not getting up)* On the table.

DUTRÉCY: *(Not moving)* All right! ...I'll get it!... *(Seeing that* THÉRÈSE *doesn't get up, he gets up.)* I'll go get it myself!... *(Aside)* She's nibbling her cookie...

AUBIN: *(Appearing)* Monsieur de la Porcheraie! *(He removes the table.)*

DUTRÉCY: *(Put out; aside)* Ah, a disturbance!

LA PORCHERAIE: *(Entering; he is very excited. To* DUTRÉCY*)* I was sure to find you in at lunchtime...

DUTRÉCY: What's the matter? You look in complete disarray...you're so calm ordinarily...

LA PORCHERAIE: Calm! ...Of course I'm calm when it concerns other people, but if you knew what's happened to me...

DUTRÉCY: What is it?

LA PORCHERAIE: Something extremely disagreeable... something unheard-of... *(Bowing to* THÉRÈSE.*)* Mademoiselle...

THÉRÈSE: I shall withdraw...

LA PORCHERAIE: *(To* THÉRÈSE*)* Sorry...it'll only take a minute...

DUTRÉCY: It'll only take a minute...

*(*THÉRÈSE *exits.)*

LA PORCHERAIE: *(To* DUTRÉCY*)* Just imagine, my dear fellow, when I got home just now… *(Noticing* AUBIN*)* What on earth are you doing over there, you?

AUBIN: I'm waiting for you to finish…I have to talk to the master too…

DUTRÉCY: *(To* AUBIN*)* Will you leave me in peace!…

AUBIN: It's just that…

DUTRÉCY: I haven't got the time to listen to you…get out!

AUBIN: *(Aside)* I've got to find time with him soon! *(He exits.)*

DUTRÉCY: All right…talk!

LA PORCHERAIE: Well, my friend… My wife is up to her old tricks…

DUTRÉCY: What?

LA PORCHERAIE: She just sent me an official notification to receive her into the conjugal domicile!

DUTRÉCY: What! a declaration of war!

LA PORCHERAIE: *(Handing a piece of official paper to* DUTRÉCY*)* Here! …This is her bombshell!

DUTRÉCY: Let's see!… *(Reading.)* Eight-hundred and sixty-four, 23 February, on the petition of Madame…

LA PORCHERAIE: Skip! Skip!

DUTRÉCY: *(Reading)* "I have stated and declared to the aforesaid monsieur de la Porcheraie that if the petitioner has dwelt for some years separated *de facto* from the aforesaid monsieur de la Porcheraie, it was the result of a mutual agreement between the latter and the said petitioner. That Madame de la Porcheraie intends today to re-establish co-habitation…"

LA PORCHERAIE: What can have come over her, after eleven years of untroubled separation?

DUTRÉCY: "That, however, if Monsieur de la Porcheraie refuses to receive her, this refusal is without merit, since it is based on no legitimate cause. That in effect, no physical separation was legally pronounced between the two spouses. That by terms of Article 214 of the Napoleonic Code, the wife has the right to cohabit with her husband and follow him wherever he considers it suitable to reside."

LA PORCHERAIE: That's a bit arbitrary!...

DUTRÉCY: *(Reading)* "Consequently, I the undersigned bailiff issue a summons to the said Monsieur de la Porcheraie..."

LA PORCHERAIE: Skip! Skip!...

DUTRÉCY: *(Reading)* "And lest he have no knowledge of it, I have deposited the present copy at the cost of five francs, ninety centimes." *(Spoken)* That's reasonable! ... Five francs, ninety centimes!...

LA PORCHERAIE: So what do you advise me to do? First, I refuse to receive the petitioner! ...I won't have the petitioner under any circumstances!

DUTRÉCY: But if article 214...

LA PORCHERAIE: Article 215 ought to cancel it out. If not that one, then another one... We just have to find it... What a mistake to get married before studying law!...

DUTRÉCY: It's very simple! ...Go and consult a lawyer.

LA PORCHERAIE: But I don't know any...I've never sued anyone.

DUTRÉCY: Wait!... *(Going to find a book)* I have a law directory...you can get all the information from it.

LA PORCHERAIE: *(Taking the volume)* Thanks! I was so happy! ...I was just leaving Fourcinier's...

DUTRÉCY: Incidentally! Is it a done deal?

LA PORCHERAIE: Yes! …We came to an agreement at a hundred and fifty-five thousand francs!

DUTRÉCY: What! he upped it another five thousand francs?

LA PORCHERAIE: What do you expect? …He came up with an uncle…

DUTRÉCY: An uncle?

LA PORCHERAIE: Who also lived in the white cottage… with the green shutters…but it's a profitable transaction! …I told him that you were in it for fifty per cent, and he's going to come here right away to sign the deed of sale.

DUTRÉCY: But the deed isn't ready!

LA PORCHERAIE: Make haste!

DUTRÉCY: I'll draw it up while you pick out a lawyer… *(He goes off left.)*

LA PORCHERAIE: *(Leafing through the directory)* Which one to pick? *(Reading)* Goodrich…Goodwin… Goodyear… *(Spoken)* Which is the good *one*?

ARMAND: *(Entering at the back)* I've just been to see Georges…he had gone out…but I ran into his sister… what an adorable woman.

LA PORCHERAIE: Ah! it's you, is it?

ARMAND: What are you doing here?

LA PORCHERAIE: I'm looking for a lawyer…with my eyes shut. You wouldn't know one who's a… bachelor…or separated from his wife…that would be even better!

ARMAND: No.

LA PORCHERAIE: *(Rising)* I'm in a fine fix… I'll go to the law courts… I'll ask questions, I'll gather information… *(To ARMAND)* My friend, never get married…you have

no idea of the pitfalls marriage has in store... Article
214... *(He exits.)*

ARMAND: *(Alone)* What? article 214...

THÉRÈSE: Ah! I was spying on you! I saw you come
in... Well, did you see Monsieur Georges?

ARMAND: No...he had gone out...but I talked with
Madame de Verrières... Ah! Thérèse! What a heart!
What a soul! What charm!...

THÉRÈSE: Yes, but Georges...

ARMAND: He had gone out! ...Just yesterday, after the
ball, I spent more than an hour with her...she told me
her life story...a life of sacrifice and devotion!

THÉRÈSE: *(Impatient)* What about Georges?

ARMAND: He'll be back...as soon as he comes home,
she'll bring him here herself...she is so good! You have
to know her...

THÉRÈSE: So he still loves me?

ARMAND: Of course... Her manner may seem cold,
even severe...

THÉRÈSE: Then why did he refuse my hand?

ARMAND: Who?

THÉRÈSE: Georges!

ARMAND: Ah! because...no! ...I can't tell you...but he's
the most faithful and most devoted man I know...the
very brother of his sister! ...Intelligent, sensitive, kind-
hearted!...

THÉRÈSE: Georges?

ARMAND: His sister! Georges too!

THÉRÈSE: And he'll be coming here?

ARMAND: I'm waiting for them... He'll propose again,
he'll make excuses to our uncle...who will let himself

be won over...I am counting a lot on Madame de
Verrières...

THÉRÈSE: Oh, uncle will do whatever I want! ...He is
so indulgent to me...he treats me with quite fatherly
affection... Last night, when we got home, I was so
sad...he kissed my hands...

ARMAND: What? He did?

THÉRÈSE: He often does...

ARMAND: That's peculiar...and what does he say while
he kisses your hands?

THÉRÈSE: Oh, I don't dare repeat it... He tells me I'm
very sweet—and that we would live together very
happily.

ARMAND: *(Aside, repressing a suspicion)* Come, come!
Don't be absurd!

THÉRÈSE: For instance, this morning he hurt me...
without meaning to...he suspects Georges...

ARMAND: Of what?

THÉRÈSE: Of cherishing a love in his heart for
somebody else...

ARMAND: That's slander!

THÉRÈSE: He insists that a man's ideas never settle
down until he's fifty to fifty-four.

ARMAND: *(Aside)* Just his age! Right! I'll look into
this!...

(GEORGES appears at the back.)

THÉRÈSE: *(Noticing him)* Ah, there's Monsieur Georges!

GEORGES: Mademoiselle...I hesitate to make an
appearance... Forgive me...I am not as guilty as I may
seem...what I did I had to do...but I have never ceased
to love you...

THÉRÈSE: Oh, I'm sure of it!…

ARMAND: You are alone? I thought that Madame de Verrières…

GEORGES: She stayed downstairs in the carriage.

ARMAND: But why? …We need her support…I'll go and get her.

GEORGES: No…stay! …I have to talk to you!

THÉRÈSE: I'll go and ask her to come up… *(To ARMAND.)* You inform uncle…he's in his study… *(She exits at the back.)*

GEORGES: Armand, before I try a new ploy with Monsieur Dutrécy, I wanted to ask you a question which I hope you will answer honestly and sincerely.

ARMAND: Speak!

GEORGES: Is it true that you don't love Thérèse?

ARMAND: *(Quickly)* Oh, my friend, I swear it! … Certainly Thèrèse is pretty!…

GEORGES: Scrumptious! …Her eyes are so blue…

ARMAND: *(Aside)* Him too…he thinks they're blue!… *(Aloud)* But you understand…her tastes are not my tastes…her character…

GEORGES: Is charming! I don't know what you can have against her?

ARMAND: I have nothing against her…she's a child, she has the faults of her age, frivolity, thoughtlessness!

GEORGES: You're mistaken, you don't know her… Thérèse is staid, thoughtful.

ARMAND: Really! I assure you she is not!

GEORGES: And I assure you she is!

ARMAND: Look here, you're not going to pick a quarrel with me because I'm not in love with your wife?

GEORGES: Because you seem to be saying Thérèse is thoughtless…if she were to have a fault, it's rather that she's too serious…she looks down at the floor…

ARMAND: I know why that is!

GEORGES: Why?

ARMAND: Why…apparently out of modesty…

GEORGES: Ah!

ARMAND: Look! Do you want me to give you a better reason for my indifference to Thérèse?

GEORGES: Yes…because the other ones are pathetic!

ARMAND: Well, my friend…I believe I love someone else…

GEORGES: Go on! Since when?

ARMAND: Since yesterday…

GEORGES: Damn! …You don't waste time! …And may one know the object of this new passion? A very serious woman, no doubt.

ARMAND: Ah! my friend, a woman…who has no equal on this earth!…

GEORGES: Thanks for Thérèse's sake.

ARMAND: She's a widow…who has sworn never to remarry…

GEORGES: Oh fine! What are you going to do about that?

ARMAND: I'm going to love her and not tell her!

GEORGES: Good lord! You fellows in the navy are pretty weird! Suppose I spoke for you?

ARMAND: No point! …Her rank and fortune forbid me to think of her…

GEORGES: I know her?…

ARMAND: Yes!

GEORGES: Who?

ARMAND: I can't tell you...

GEORGES: Not tell *me*?...

ARMAND: Please...let me keep this secret...the only one there will ever be between us.

GEORGES: You're making a mistake refusing my services, I am very eloquent on behalf of my friends.

ARMAND: Well, try to be a little for yourself...I'll go get my uncle, and I foresee problems.

GEORGES: What sort?

ARMAND: No...I'm not sure enough yet...anyway, we shall see...wait for me!... *(He goes off left.)*

MME DE VERRIÈRES: *(Appearing at back while speaking into the wings)* It's charming! It's a marvel!

GEORGES: Who are you talking to?

MME DE VERRIÈRES: Thérèse... She is in seventh heaven! Her uncle just had her sent a magnificent lace mantilla... That uncle of hers is definitely a very good man...

GEORGES: I just had things out with Armand.

MME DE VERRIÈRES: Well? did you find him radically cured?

GEORGES: What I mean is...you don't know this...he's in love with another woman!

MME DE VERRIÈRES: *(Giving a start)* Ah!...

GEORGES: *(Aside)* Why, she was startled! ...Can it be?...

MME DE VERRIÈRES: Monsieur Armand, in love! ...What a joke!...

GEORGES: It's very serious. He didn't want to give her name. I only know she's a widow...

MME DE VERRIÈRES: Ah!

GEORGES: *(Aside)* Again! *(Aloud)* A widow who doesn't want to remarry!…

MME DE VERRIÈRES: Really?

GEORGES: And who, in addition, occupies a rather high position in society!…

MME DE VERRIÈRES: A moneyed position?

GEORGES: *(Watching her)* Yes…she's the widow…of an admiral.

MME DE VERRIÈRES: Good heavens!

GEORGES: *(Quickly)* No, a colonel! …You love him!…

MME DE VERRIÈRES: Be still! …I didn't say a thing!…

GEORGES: I heard you!…Well, kiss me!…

THÉRÈSE: *(Entering)* Ah, isn't uncle good to me! He picked out the most expensive thing! Here he is!…

(ARMAND and DUTRÉCY enter.)

ARMAND: Come in, uncle.

DUTRÉCY: *(Bowing)* Madame…Monsieur Georges…I confess I did not expect you to pay a visit after yesterday's scandal.

MME DE VERRIÈRES: Indeed, my brother did not dare present himself…I was the one who brought him…

GEORGES: Monsieur Dutrécy…please accept my apology…I lost my head a bit…I thought I was doing my duty…fortunately, I was mistaken… So I come now and ask you to put me back in your good graces… and remake the promise you gave me…

DUTRÉCY: My dear Monsieur Georges…you see me most distressed…but after your renunciation…I had to believe myself free…and I have promised Thérèse's hand to someone else.

ALL: What?

THÉRÈSE: *(Undertone)* Another suitor? I won't have him!...

DUTRÉCY: *(Undertone)* Thérèse, be still!...

THÉRÈSE: *(Undertone)* You promised to grant me whatever I asked you...

DUTRÉCY: *(Undertone)* Do you want me to send you back to Mademoiselle Pinta?

THÉRÈSE: *(Undertone)* No!

DUTRÉCY: *(Undertone)* Then keep still!

GEORGES: Please, Monsieur, do not destroy my fondest hopes by a refusal...it is impossible that in so short a time you have committed yourself so irrevocably...

DUTRÉCY: Irrevocably!

GEORGES: Might I at least know the individual?

DUTRÉCY: He is a man who has all my sympathies... who will make my niece happy, I am sure of it...but I cannot yet give you his name...

ARMAND: *(Aside)* It's him!... *(Aloud)* Uncle, may I say two words to you in private?

DUTRÉCY: To me? Of course, my friend.

ARMAND: *(To the others)* May I? ...Just one minute...

MME DE VERRIÈRES: *(Aside)* What is he up to?

DUTRÉCY: Thérèse...go to your room!

THÉRÈSE: Oh! how you have changed, uncle!

(GEORGES, MME DE VERRIÈRES go off left, Thérèse exits at the back.)

ARMAND: *(Aside)* If he loves Thérèse...I shall find it out!...

DUTRÉCY: *(Aside)* What the devil does he want with me?

ARMAND: Ah, uncle! I was eager to be alone with you… and now I don't know how to thank you…I lack the words to express my gratitude.

DUTRÉCY: To me? …What for?

ARMAND: I remember what you told me yesterday at the ball… "To marry you to Thérèse…has been my dream!"

DUTRÉCY: Excuse me!

ARMAND: Oh, I saw right through you… This husband who is to make Thérèse happy…who has all your sympathies…it's me!

DUTRÉCY: *(Quickly)* No! don't get carried away!…

ARMAND: You didn't want to make sport of me…what you said to me yesterday…

DUTRÉCY: Certainly, you're a good-natured fellow… I'm very fond of you…but you have no fortune…no position…

ARMAND: Oh, with my wife's dowry, I shall know how to get one…

DUTRÉCY: Your wife! …Your wife! …I tell you not to get carried away!…

ARMAND: How can one resist so many charms? If you were to know her…for I am sure you've paid her no attention!…

DUTRÉCY: Yes I have!

ARMAND: *(Aside)* Ah!… *(Aloud)* She is so beautiful!

DUTRÉCY: With her blue eyes!

ARMAND: *(Aside)* Love must wear blue-tinted glasses! *(Aloud)* And her voice! What sweetness! And her hands!

DUTRÉCY: Yes, yes! ...And her feet! ...You can't hear her footfall...you feel her pass by...like a breath of air! Like a breeze whose cool breath...

ARMAND: *(Interrupting him)* Come now! Don't mince words! You love her!...

DUTRÉCY: *(Quickly)* I never said that!...

ARMAND: You're blushing! There's something in it!

DUTRÉCY: I am not blushing!

ARMAND: Then, uncle, I feel sorry for you...such a piece of folly...

DUTRÉCY: Monsieur Armand, I don't need any advice from you.

ARMAND: Nevertheless allow me to offer you some... respectfully...but with the firm intention of opposing your plans.

DUTRÉCY: What, I can't get married if I choose! And these people invade my house!... *(Calming down.)* No...I won't lose my temper...Forcinier forbade me to... And these people invade my house...but you will find that I can do without your advice...I shall do what I believe best, and I shall not give in to your entreaties or your threats...

ARMAND: We shall see...

DUTRÉCY: And after what I have just said, I do not need to add: now that I find my house too cramped, you can from today choose another residence...

ARMAND: Very well, since you give me my freedom, I shall take advantage of it... You want a fight? All right! I accept.

DUTRÉCY: Huh?

(GEORGES *and* MME DE VERRIÈRES *appear.)*

ARMAND: Come in! …Everything must take place in the clear light of day!…

DUTRÉCY: What is he up to?

ARMAND: You do not know the suitor for the hand of our dear Thérèse?

DUTRÉCY: Later!

ARMAND: May I introduce him to you. *(He points to* DUTRÉCY.*)*

MME DE VERRIÈRES: Monsieur Dutrécy!

GEORGES: Him!

ARMAND: *(Undertone to* DUTRÉCY*)* You see the effect!…

GEORGES: But, Monsieur, that's impossible!

DUTRÉCY: And why is that, Monsieur, if I may ask?

GEORGES: You don't love her…you can't love her…at your age…whereas I…if you take her away from me, I'll die!

DUTRÉCY: Well, I'd die as well! and I would rather it be you. *(Aside)* I have to get rid of all these people!…

*(*AUBIN *appears.)*

DUTRÉCY: Call a cab…you will come back and get the trunks of Monsieur Armand who is leaving…

GEORGES: *(To* ARMAND*)* They're throwing you out… come to my place…your place!

AUBIN: *(Aside)* More trunks! *(To* DUTRÉCY*)* I have something important to tell Monsieur…

DUTRÉCY: Later!

ARMAND: *(To* DUTRÉCY*)* I won't say good-bye, uncle, we shall meet again! …Thank you, Georges, come… *(He goes into his room with* GEORGES.*)*

DUTRÉCY: *(Aside)* This is beyond belief! To come and challenge me…in my own home!…

MME DE VERRIÈRES: Monsieur Dutrécy...

DUTRÉCY: *(Aside)* Oh dear, the sister's still here...
(Aloud) Madame...

MME DE VERRIÈRES: I still hope to make you give up a
project...which is unreasonable...

DUTRÉCY: Excuse me, Madame, I'm old enough to
know what I'm doing...

MME DE VERRIÈRES: Exactly... consider your age and
that of Thérèse.

DUTRÉCY. My health is excellent...and I take marvelous
care of myself!

MME DE VERRIÈRES: Monsieur Dutrécy...please listen
to me! You don't know the pain you are about to inflict
on this child. I too was married young...to a gallant
man...the same as you...

DUTRÉCY: Madame! *(Aside)* At least she's polite!

MME DE VERRIÈRES: Colonel de Verrières, my husband,
was twenty-two years older than I...

DUTRÉCY: There is not so much between Thérèse and
me.

MME DE VERRIÈRES: They say you're fifty-four.

DUTRÉCY: Barely!

MME DE VERRIÈRES: Thérèse is nineteen.

DUTRÉCY: And a half!

MME DE VERRIÈRES: That makes thirty-five years...

DUTRÉCY: *(Quickly)* I don't know that! I can't do math
in my head!

MME DE VERRIÈRES: Very well! Monsieur, I am going to
confess...something I have never told anyone...I was
not happy with my husband...

DUTRÉCY: Ah! sorry, but what about *him*?

MME DE VERRIÈRES: Oh, he was unaware of it...I lavished care...attention...affectionate concern on him...

DUTRÉCY: *(To himself)* Well, what's wrong with that?

MME DE VERRIÈRES: But I did not find in his heart what there was in mine...youth...spirit...aspiration...

DUTRÉCY: Oh that!...

MME DE VERRIÈRES: Monsieur de Verrières' tastes were not mine...he was ending and I was beginning... Nevertheless I did my duty...sacrificed my desires...

DUTRÉCY: *(To himself)* What of it? ...She's quite a nice lady!

MME DE VERRIÈRES: My husband was afflicted with gout!

DUTRÉCY: Is that so!

MME DE VERRIÈRES: When I was at the age of diversions and pleasures, I had to resign myself to sharing his lot. I spent the five best years of my life caring for an old man who was demanding, morose...often unjust...I never left his side, I smiled beside his pillow...only to weep when I was alone...

DUTRÉCY: Poor woman! What about *him*...was he happy?

MME DE VERRIÈRES: Oh! until his very last moment!...

DUTRÉCY: *(To himself)* So what's the problem? *(Aloud)* Madame, I thank you for those good words...I needed to hear them.

MME DE VERRIÈRES: Ah! I knew I would end up convincing you.

DUTRÉCY: Yes, I am convinced...and all I ask of heaven is that Thérèse will be as accomplished and as devoted a wife as you have been, Madame...

MME DE VERRIÈRES: What, Monsieur, after what I just
confided in you...

DUTRÉCY: What I've needed all along is a family...
Please, Madame, accept the expression of my sincere
admiration and my profound respect...

MME DE VERRIÈRES: *(Drily)* Thank you... May I say
good-bye to Thérèse?

DUTRÉCY: But of course! Thérèse can take only good
examples in your company!

MME DE VERRIÈRES: *(Aside)* What a horrid fellow! *(She
goes into* THÉRÈSE's *room.)*

DUTRÉCY: *(Alone)* Charming woman! after all, that
colonel was a happy man! And I shall be like him, in
the teeth of Monsieur Armand. He's taking his time
moving out...he's plotting with his friend... Now
we're at war...that bothers me...I don't like fights,
no indeed...they upset my serenity...my habits...my
digestion...I have to find some way...a quiet one...

LA PORCHERAIE: *(Entering suddenly)* Ah, there you are!

DUTRÉCY: *(Aside)* De la Porcheraie! Again!

LA PORCHERAIE: Ah, my friend, let me sit down! *(He
sits.)*

DUTRÉCY: What's happened?

LA PORCHERAIE: A disaster! A landslide! My wife has
come back! She has moved back in!

DUTRÉCY: *(Aside)* Ah! if that's all it is!...

LA PORCHERAIE: When I got home, I found her
ensconced in my house with her servants, her parcels
and a lapdog...which bites! They have violated my
hearth and home!

DUTRÉCY: Well, it's not as bad as all that...I have a lot
worse worries myself! ...When you've taken Madame

de la Porcheraie dancing two or three times... Can you imagine that Thérèse...

LA PORCHERAIE: Dancing indeed! That's not it! ...She's got religion!

DUTRÉCY: Religion! ...Can you imagine...

LA PORCHERAIE: People have convinced her that the only God-fearing way to live is under the conjugal roof.

DUTRÉCY: You can't be too hard on them... Can you imagine that Thérèse...

LA PORCHERAIE: *(Rising)* I ask you, how dare they meddle! ...Some people have a mania for destroying families by bringing wives home!

DUTRÉCY: For heaven's sake, calm down!

LA PORCHERAIE: You want me to be calm when in my vestibule I tripped over three sextons and a pew-opener. —Come now, do you know any way out?

DUTRÉCY: I'm looking for one... *(Aside)* If I could send Armand back to America!

LA PORCHERAIE: And my racy etchings! It's too much! You know what a collector I am!

DUTRÉCY: Yes.

LA PORCHERAIE: All those naked gods and goddesses...

DUTRÉCY: A bachelor's collection... *(Aside)* No...he'd refuse.

LA PORCHERAIE: My wife just turned them around... face to the wall.

DUTRÉCY: What did you do?

LA PORCHERAIE: I turned them back face to the world!

DUTRÉCY: Then what did she do?

La Porcheraie: She lifted her eyes to the ceiling, it's her habit now, she's always like that…so I'm going to have a mural painted on it…the ceiling…I'm going to rub her face in a Rape of Europa and an Abduction of Helen of Troy.

Dutrécy: I'd come and see that… Ah, I've got it!

La Porcheraie: What?

Dutrécy: The way out! …A trip! …I'll take her away! …I'll abduct her!…

La Porcheraie: My wife?… *(Thanking him.)* My dear friend!

Dutrécy: No, my niece! As her guardian, I have the right!

La Porcheraie: What are we playing at now? I'm talking about my wife…

Dutrécy: And I'm talking about Thérèse!…

La Porcheraie: Thérèse! What's that got to do with me?

Dutrécy: Well, what has your wife got to do with *me*? I can't constantly be bothered with your affairs…you've got to be reasonable.

La Porcheraie: That's fair…so you have things on your mind as well?

Dutrécy: Yes… Can you imagine that Thérèse…

La Porcheraie: First I want to exhaust every means of reconciliation in order to separate us…

Dutrécy: But I am delighted with my idea…because a trip…

La Porcheraie: Someone recommended a lawyer who's very up-to-date…he's pleaded against his own wife…

Dutrécy: We'll leave this very evening…

LA PORCHERAIE: An astonishing fellow for divorces.

DUTRÉCY: Mysteriously…at dusk.

LA PORCHERAIE: He could separate Romeo and Juliet.

DUTRÉCY: Without luggage, as if going for a stroll.

LA PORCHERAIE: I am to see him at five o'clock.

DUTRÉCY: Aubin can join us later with the trunks.

LA PORCHERAIE: *(Pulling out his watch)* Four fifty-two!

DUTRÉCY: And in that way…

LA PORCHERAIE: I'm off… *(He exits quickly.)*

DUTRÉCY: *(Alone, continuing)* And in that way… informing no one of our itinerary…and hiding our address from everyone, I shall put any pursuers off the track…

(FOURCINIER enters at the back.)

DUTRÉCY *(Noticing him)* Why, it's the doctor!

FOURCINIER: *(Giving his hand to DUTRÉCY)* Yes, here I am!

DUTRÉCY: *(Aside)* Right on cue.

FOURCINIER: I've come for the deed of sale.

DUTRÉCY: The deed of sale?

FOURCINIER: The garden.

DUTRÉCY: Ah, the garden! You're getting a great deal there!

FOURCINIER: At a price.

DUTRÉCY: Well! in return I should like to ask a little favor.

FOURCINIER: What is it?

DUTRÉCY: Take a look at my niece and prescribe her a season at a spa.

FOURCINIER: Which spa?

DUTRÉCY: Oh, whichever you like…the spa at Spa, for instance…it's always done me a world of good!

FOURCINIER: Is she ill?

DUTRÉCY: No…I'll be the one taking the waters…but I wish to remove Thérèse from certain pursuers who are pestering me…in short, we have to go away!

FOURCINIER: Nothing simpler!

DUTRÉCY: I'll ask you for a prescription…that'll look more serious…

FOURCINIER: Very well…I shall examine Thérèse.

DUTRÉCY: Thanks! She's in her room…I shall go and get our deed of sale! …Happy doctor! What will he do with all that money? …Back in a minute…the spa at Spa, you understand? *(He exits.)*

FOURCINIER: Don't worry! …What pursuers does he want to remove Thérèse from? …After all, it's none of my business…we'll say Spa! …The mineral waters have done no one any harm.

GEORGES: *(Entering)* The trunks are packed!… *(Calling)* Aubin!

FOURCINIER: Monsieur Georges!…

GEORGES: You, Doctor! …Is someone here ill?

FOURCINIER: No. I'm here on business…I'm selling my garden in Passy to de la Porcheraie and Dutrécy.

GEORGES: What! Your garden on Rue des Dames?…

FOURCINIER: Four whole acres…a hundred and fifty-five thousand francs…that's a fine price!

GEORGES: Don't do it, it would be stupid!

FOURCINIER: How so?

GEORGES: Don't you know that they're going to put in a new street that will cross the whole length of your land? ...It's worth six hundred thousand francs.

FOURCINIER: Six hundred thousand! ...Ah! the crooks... but are you sure of this?

GEORGES: People came and offered us the deal...I refused on your account...I was going to write to you...

FOURCINIER: Ah, my friend! ...Another fifteen minutes...I would have been caught... Now I understand the business about the slaughterhouse!

GEORGES: What slaughterhouse?

FOURCINIER: Ah! I'm lying in wait for him and his deed! He'll find out what I think of him! ...An appalling man!

GEORGES: Yes! Who has taken it into his head to make love to his niece!

FOURCINIER: What? Thérèse?

GEORGES: He wants to marry her!

FOURCINIER: He! a gentleman who's trying to swindle me out of my land! ...She would be unhappy in this house!

GEORGES: Of course she would!

FOURCINIER: For you don't know him...I listen to his heart-beat every Wednesday...he's a monomaniac, a despot, an egotist who thinks only of himself...and my land...my land's worth six hundred thousand francs! ...And he has the gall to offer me...

GEORGES: I hear him.

FOURCINIER: Just as well! I shall give him a piece of my mind.

GEORGES: *(Withdrawing)* Calm down, Doctor... *(Aside)* Let them settle it between them! *(He exits.)*

DUTRÉCY: *(Entering)* Here's our little deed of sale...we shall just run over it.

FOURCINIER: *(Aside, looking at him)* And *that* wants to get married! What an idea...really!

DUTRÉCY: "Between the undersigned..."

FOURCINIER: Wait... I'll be right with you... *(He sits down at the table and writes.)*

DUTRÉCY: You're writing the prescription?

FOURCINIER: Yes... *(Aside, while writing.)* Ah! I'll teach you to toss slaughterhouses into doctor's gardens!...

DUTRÉCY: You put down Spa?

FOURCINIER: Don't worry. *(Rising)* But first, my dear Dutrécy, give me your hand...what you're doing is a good idea.

DUTRÉCY: What's that?

FOURCINIER: I've just learned of your marriage to Thérèse.

DUTRÉCY: Ah! and you don't disapprove too much!

FOURCINIER: Not at all!

DUTRÉCY: And as to my state of health...you don't see any problems there?

FOURCINIER: None!

DUTRÉCY: Very good! So I shall continue my present regimen.

FOURCINIER: My friend, excuse me, I never gave you credit...it's fine! It's grand! ...In the name of humanity, I thank you!

DUTRÉCY: Why in the name of humanity?

FOURCINIER: As you suggested, I have just seen Thérèse…I did not find her well…

DUTRÉCY: *(Astonished)* What?…

FOURCINIER: Oh, not at all well!

DUTRÉCY: How so!…

FOURCINIER: You're right, she has a sickly nature… underdeveloped…languid…

DUTRÉCY: She's never been sick a day in her life!

FOURCINIER: Don't you believe it! …Tell me…did she undergo a shock today, something untoward?…

DUTRÉCY: Yes! …We had a little scene…

FOURCINIER: There you are! But sooner or later it's bound to happen…

DUTRÉCY: But what has she got?

FOURCINIER: My friend, her entire constitution has got to be rehabilitated!

DUTRÉCY: As bad as that!…

FOURCINIER: A weak heart, hyper-sensitive nerves… impressionability of the mucous membrane…

DUTRÉCY: Then there's nothing sound about her!…

FOURCINIER: It will go on a long time…a long, long time.

DUTRÉCY: How long a time, more or less?

FOURCINIER: Four years…six years…ten years! You never know! She's a woman who will drag out her life…

DUTRÉCY: So she'll have to undergo constant treatment?

FOURCINIER: Here's the prescription… I'll come back this evening.

DUTRÉCY: *(Taking the prescription)* In other words I'm going to be a nurse!

FOURCINIER: Ah…I was forgetting…you'll have to spend the winter in Malta, perhaps Egypt…

DUTRÉCY: Egypt! …At my age! …Where is Georges? Has Georges left?

(Seeing GEORGES *enter with* ARMAND:*)*

DUTRÉCY: He hasn't left… Come in! Come closer, my friend…my dear Georges!

GEORGES: What is it, Monsieur Dutrécy?

DUTRÉCY: Wait!…

FOURCINIER: The effect of my prescription!…

DUTRÉCY: *(Going to the door left)* Thérèse! …Madame! … You are going to find out what sort of man I am.

THÉRÈSE: What's the matter, uncle?

DUTRÉCY: My children, an uncle's heart is practically that of a father; I no longer wish to oppose a true affection. Georges! …I remake my promise!

ALL: What?

GEORGES & MME DE VERRIÈRES: Ah! Monsieur Dutrécy!…

ARMAND: Someone has changed his mind!

THÉRÈSE & ARMAND: Ah, Uncle!… *(They gather around* DUTRÉCY *and congratulate him.)*

FOURCINIER: *(Aside, downstage)* He ought to have his portrait painted like that!…

DUTRÉCY: I too know how to make a sacrifice when need be…

MME DE VERRIÈRES: Monsieur Dutrécy, you have regained my respect.

DUTRÉCY: Ah, Madame!… *(Undertone to* FOURCINIER.*)*
This is the woman who will do the job…kind…
devoted…in good health!… *(Aside)* I have to have a
word with Fromental…as a Saint-Barbian…Madame…

ARMAND: Good-bye, Uncle!

DUTRÉCY: What?

ARMAND: Georges is happy…I can depart…

DUTRÉCY: Where are you going?

ARMAND: To New York!…

MME DE VERRIÈRES: What!

GEORGES: No…I forbid it.

ARMAND: Why?

GEORGES: My sister doesn't want her husband to travel
without her…

MME DE VERRIÈRES: Georges!

ARMAND: What are you saying?

GEORGES: Indeed she doesn't! …You love one
another!…

ARMAND: Madame? …Ah, Uncle!… *(He throws himself
into* DUTRÉCY's *arms.)*

DUTRÉCY: *(Aside)* Too late! I am losing a delightful
woman…but I still have a family to look after me…

THÉRÈSE: Oh, dear uncle, be happy and enjoy the
happiness you have given me.

DUTRÉCY: Yes, my child!…

THÉRÈSE: After the ceremony, we shall leave for
Switzerland…all four of us!

ALL. Yes! yes! how charming!

DUTRÉCY: Switzerland!…

MME DE VERRIÈRES: My carriage is downstairs… Let us go and announce the good news to my father.

(They exit.)

DUTRÉCY: *(To* FOURCINIER*)* They are abandoning me… after all I've done for them!…

FOURCINIER: How dreadful!

*(*AUBIN *appears.)*

DUTRÉCY: Aubin! Devotion itself! Innocent Brittany! Come near, my friend: you care for me, don't you?…

AUBIN: *(Confused)* Shucks! …A little bit…

DUTRÉCY: You had something to tell me; what do you want?

AUBIN: *(Confused)* I wanted to ask Monsieur…if Monsieur would be so kind as to…send me away from Monsieur!

DUTRÉCY: What! you want to leave me!

AUBIN: I've found a job as concierge… *(He makes the gesture of pulling a cord.)* I'd be in charge…with a hundred francs more…

DUTRÉCY: *(Disgusted)* Oh!

AUBIN: In an airier part of town…and shucks! as Monsieur is fond of saying…you can't take too much care of yourself…

DUTRÉCY: *(Quickly)* Enough! …I won't hold you back!… *(Aside)* Not much of Brittany's innocence left!…

*(*DE LA PORCHERAIE *enters in travelling clothes.)*

AUBIN: *(Exiting)* Monsieur de la Porcheraie!

DUTRÉCY: De la Porcheraie! …I won't be alone after all!

LA PORCHERAIE: My dear fellow, I'm leaving…

DUTRÉCY: What?

LA PORCHERAIE: My wife has indeed the legal right to live in my home… So, I no longer wish to have a home…I am going to travel…I will defend myself by flight.

DUTRÉCY: And you come to me to say your fond farewells!

LA PORCHERAIE: No! I came for the deed of sale!…

DUTRÉCY: Ah, yes…the deed of sale! …Let's sign it…

FOURCINIER: Later…when the street is built… *(He exits.)*

LA PORCHERAIE: He's a sharp operator!

DUTRÉCY: Totally dishonest!

LA PORCHERAIE: The train's about to leave, I'm going.

DUTRÉCY: We'll write one another…

LA PORCHERAIE: What's the point? We've nothing to say to one another!

DUTRÉCY: But we'll never see one another again!

LA PORCHERAIE: So what! Does that mean anything to you?

DUTRÉCY: Well! what about you?

LA PORCHERAIE: Me! …Nothing at all. *(He exits.)*

DUTRÉCY: *(Alone)* Ah! the human race! The human race! Ultimately there's no one I can love but me!

(Curtain)

END OF PLAY

www.ingramcontent.com/pod-product-compliance
Lightning Source LLC
Chambersburg PA
CBHW052150090426
42741CB00010B/2208